W9-ASB-682

MAN'S SEARCH FOR MEANING

an introduction to logotherapy

A NEWLY REVISED AND ENLARGED
EDITION OF

from DEATH-CAMP

to Existentialism

BY VIKTOR E. FRANKL

Translated by Ilse Lasch

Preface by Gordon W. Allport

A TOUCHSTONE BOOK

PUBLISHED BY SIMON AND SCHUSTER

To the memory of my mother

Copyright © 1959 by Viktor Frankl
Revised edition copyright © 1962 by Viktor Frankl
All rights reserved
including the right of reproduction
in whole or in part in any form
Reprinted by arrangement with Beacon Press

A Touchstone Book
Published by Simon and Schuster
A Division of Gulf & Western Corporation
Simon & Schuster Building
Rockefeller Center, 1230 Avenue of the Americas
New York, New York 10020

ISBN 0-671-20782-2

First published in Austria in 1946, under the title *Ein Psycholog erlebt das Konzentrationslager*. This translation first published by Beacon Press in 1959. Beacon Press books are published under the auspices of the Unitarian Universalist Association.

Manufactured in the United States of America
7 8 9 10 11 12 13 14 15

Contents

Preface

Dr. Frankl, author-psychiatrist, sometimes asks his patients who suffer from a multitude of torments great and small, "Why do you not commit suicide?" From their answers he can often find the guide-line for his psychotherapy: in one life there is love for one's children to tie to; in another life, a talent to be used; in a third, perhaps only lingering memories worth preserving. To weave these slender threads of a broken life into a firm pattern of meaning and responsibility is the object and challenge of *logotherapy*, which is Dr. Frankl's own version of modern *existential analysis*.

In this book, Dr. Frankl explains the experience which led to his discovery of logotherapy. As a longtime prisoner in bestial concentration camps he found himself stripped to naked existence. His father, mother, brother, and his wife died in camps or were sent to the gas ovens, so that, excepting for his sister, his entire family perished in these camps. How could he—every possession lost, every value destroyed, suffering from hunger, cold and brutality, hourly expecting extermination—how could he find life worth preserving? A psychiatrist who personally has faced such extremity is a psychiatrist worth listening to. He, if anyone, should be able to view our human condition wisely and with compassion. Dr. Frankl's words have a profoundly honest ring, for they rest on experiences too deep for deception. What he has to say gains in prestige because of his present position on the Medical Faculty of the Univer-

sity of Vienna and because of the renown of the logotherapy clinics that today are springing up in many lands,
patterned on his own famous Neurological Policlinic in
Vienna.

One cannot help but compare Viktor Frankl's approach to theory and therapy with the work of his prede-
cessor, Sigmund Freud. Both physicians concern themselves primarily with the nature and cure of neuroses.
Freud finds the root of these distressing disorders in the
anxiety caused by conflicting and unconscious motives.
Frankl distinguishes several forms of neurosis, and traces
some of them (the noögenic neuroses) to the failure of the
sufferer to find meaning and a sense of responsibility in his
existence. Freud stresses frustration in the sexual life;
Frankl, frustration in the "will-to-meaning." In Europe
today there is a marked turning away from Freud and a
widespread embracing of existential analysis, which takes
several related forms—the school of logotherapy being one.
It is characteristic of Frankl's tolerant outlook that he does
not repudiate Freud, but builds gladly on his contributions;
nor does he quarrel with other forms of existential therapy,
but welcomes kinship with them.

The present narrative, brief though it is, is artfully
constructed and gripping. On two occasions I have read it
through at a single sitting, unable to break away from its
spell. Somewhere beyond the midpoint of the story Dr.
Frankl introduces his own philosophy of logotherapy. He
introduces it so gently into the continuing narrative that
only after finishing the book does the reader realize that
here is an essay of profound depth, and not just one more
brutal tale of concentration camps.

From this autobiographical fragment the reader
learns much. He learns what a human being does
when he suddenly realizes he has "nothing to lose except

his so ridiculously naked life." Frankl's description of the mixed flow of emotion and apathy is arresting. First to the rescue comes a cold detached curiosity concerning one's fate. Swiftly, too, come strategies to preserve the remnants of one's life, though the chances of surviving are slight. Hunger, humiliation, fear and deep anger at injustice are rendered tolerable by closely guarded images of beloved persons, by religion, by a grim sense of humor, and even by glimpses of the healing beauties of nature—a tree or a sunset.

But these moments of comfort do not establish the will to live unless they help the prisoner make larger sense out of his apparently senseless suffering. It is here that we encounter the central theme of existentialism: to live is to suffer, to survive is to find meaning in the suffering. If there is a purpose in life at all, there must be a purpose in suffering and in dying. But no man can tell another what this purpose is. Each must find out for himself, and must accept the responsibility that his answer prescribes. If he succeeds he will continue to grow in spite of all indignities. Frankl is fond of quoting Nietzsche, "He who has a *why* to live can bear with almost any *how*."

In the concentration camp every circumstance conspires to make the prisoner lose his hold. All the familiar goals in life are snatched away. What alone remains is "the last of human freedoms"—the ability to "choose one's attitude in a given set of circumstances." This ultimate freedom, recognized by the ancient Stoics as well as by modern existentialists, takes on vivid significance in Frankl's story. The prisoners were only average men, but some, at least, by choosing to be "worthy of their suffering" proved man's capacity to rise above his outward fate.

As a psychotherapist, the author, of course, wants to know how men can be helped to achieve this distinctively human capacity. How can one awaken in a patient the feeling that he is responsible to life for something, however grim his circumstances may be? Frankl gives us a moving account of one collective therapeutic session he held with his fellow prisoners.

At the publisher's request Dr. Frankl has added a statement of the basic tenets of logotherapy as well as a bibliography. Up to now most of the publications of this "Third Viennese School of Psychotherapy" (the predecessors being the Freudian and Adlerian Schools) have been chiefly in German. The reader will therefore welcome Dr. Frankl's supplement to his personal narrative.

Unlike many European existentialists, Frankl is neither pessimistic nor antireligious. On the contrary, for a writer who faces fully the ubiquity of suffering and the forces of evil, he takes a surprisingly hopeful view of man's capacity to transcend his predicament and discover an adequate guiding truth.

I recommend this little book heartily, for it is a gem of dramatic narrative, focused upon the deepest of human problems. It has literary and philosophical merit and provides a compelling introduction to the most significant psychological movement of our day.

GORDON W. ALLPORT

Gordon W. Allport, formerly a professor of psychology at Harvard University, was one of the foremost writers and teachers in the field in this hemisphere. He was author of a large number of original works on psychology and was the editor of the *Journal of Abnormal and Social Psychology*. It is chiefly through the pioneering work of Professor Allport that Dr. Frankl's momentous theory was introduced to this country; moreover, it is to his credit that the interest shown here in logotherapy is growing by leaps and bounds.

Part One

Experiences in a
Concentration Camp

This book does not claim to be an account of facts and events but of personal experiences, experiences which millions of prisoners have suffered time and again. It is the inside story of a concentration camp, told by one of its survivors. This tale is not concerned with the great horrors, which have already been described often enough (though less often believed), but with the multitude of small torments. In other words, it will try to answer this question: How was everyday life in a concentration camp reflected in the mind of the average prisoner?

Most of the events described here did not take place in the large and famous camps, but in the small ones where most of the real extermination took place. This story is not about the suffering and death of great heroes and martyrs, nor is it about the prominent Capos—prisoners who acted as trustees, having special privileges—or well-known prisoners. Thus it is not so much concerned with the sufferings of the mighty, but with the sacrifices, the crucifixion and the deaths of the great army of unknown and unrecorded victims. It was these common prisoners, who bore no distinguishing marks on their sleeves, whom the Capos really despised. While these ordinary prisoners had little or nothing to eat, the Capos were never hungry; in fact many of the Capos fared better in the camp than they had in their entire lives. Often they were harder on the prisoners than were the guards, and beat them more cruelly than the SS men did. These Capos, of course, were chosen only from those prisoners whose characters promised to make them suitable for such procedures, and if they did not comply with what was expected of them, they were immediately demoted. They soon became much like the SS men and the camp wardens and may be judged on a similar psychological basis.

It is easy for the outsider to get the wrong conception of camp life, a conception mingled with sentiment and pity. Little does he know of the hard fight for existence which raged among the prisoners. This was an unrelenting struggle for daily bread and for life itself, for one's own sake or for that of a good friend.

Let us take the case of a transport which was officially announced to transfer a certain number of prisoners to another camp; but it was a fairly safe guess that its final destination would be the gas chambers. A selection of sick or feeble prisoners incapable of work would be sent to one of the big central camps which were fitted with gas chambers and crematoriums. The selection process was the signal for a free fight among all the prisoners, or of group against group. All that mattered was that one's own name and that of one's friend were crossed off the list of victims, though everyone knew that for each man saved another victim had to be found.

A definite number of prisoners had to go with each transport. It did not really matter which, since each of them was nothing but a number. On their admission to the camp (at least this was the method in Auschwitz) all their documents had been taken from them, together with their other possessions. Each prisoner, therefore, had had an opportunity to claim a fictitious name or profession; and for various reasons many did this. The authorities were interested only in the captives' numbers. These numbers were often tattooed on their skin, and also had to be sewn to a certain spot on the trousers, jacket, or coat. Any guard who wanted to make a charge against a prisoner just glanced at his number (and how we dreaded such glances!); he never asked for his name.

To return to the convoy about to depart. There was neither time nor desire to consider moral or ethical issues. Every man was controlled by one thought only: to keep himself alive for the family waiting for him at home, and to save his friends. With no hesitation, therefore, he would arrange for another prisoner, another "number," to take his place in the transport.

As I have already mentioned, the process of selecting Capos was a negative one; only the most brutal of the prisoners were chosen for this job (although there were some happy exceptions). But apart from the selection of Capos which was undertaken by the SS, there was a sort of self-selecting process going on the whole time among all of the prisoners. On the average, only those prisoners could keep alive who, after years of trekking from camp to camp, had lost all scruples in their fight for existence; they were prepared to use every means, honest and otherwise, even brutal force, theft, and betrayal of their friends, in order to save themselves. We who have come back, by the aid of many lucky chances or miracles—whatever one may choose to call them—we know: the best of us did not return.

Many factual accounts about concentration camps are already on record. Here, facts will be significant only as far as they are part of a man's experiences. It is the exact nature of these experiences that the following essay will attempt to describe. For those who have been inmates in a camp, it will attempt to explain their experiences in the light of present-day knowledge. And for those who have never been inside, it may help them to comprehend, and above all to understand, the experiences of that only too small percentage of prisoners who survived and who now find life very difficult. These former prisoners often say, "We dislike talking about our experiences. No explanations are needed for those who have been inside, and the others will understand neither how we felt then nor how we feel now."

To attempt a methodical presentation of the subject is very difficult, as psychology requires a certain scientific detachment. But does a man who makes his observations while he himself is a prisoner possess the necessary detachment? Such detachment is granted to the outsider, but he is too far removed to make any statements of real value. Only the man inside knows. His judgments may not be objective; his evaluations may be out of proportion. This is inevitable. An attempt must be made to avoid any personal bias, and that is the real difficulty of a book of this kind. At times it will be necessary to have the courage to tell of very intimate experiences. I had intended to write this book anonymously, using my prison number only. But when the manuscript was completed, I saw that as an anonymous publication it would lose half its value, and that I must have the courage to state my convictions openly. I therefore refrained from deleting any of the passages, in spite of an intense dislike of exhibitionism.

I shall leave it to others to distill the contents of this book into dry theories. These might become a contribution to the psychology of prison life, which was investigated after the First World War, and which acquainted us with the syndrome of "barbed wire sickness." We are indebted to the Second World War for enriching our knowledge of the "psychopathology of the masses," (if I may quote a variation of the well-known phrase and title of a book by LeBon), for the war gave us the war of nerves and it gave us the concentration camp.

As this story is about my experiences as an ordinary prisoner, it is important that I mention, not without pride, that I was not employed as a psychiatrist in camp, or even as a doctor, except for the last few weeks. A few of my colleagues were lucky enough to be employed in poorly heated first-aid posts applying bandages made of scraps of waste paper. But I was Number 119,104, and most of the time I was digging and laying tracks for railway lines. At one time, my job was to dig a tunnel, without help, for a water main under a road. This feat did not go unrewarded; just before Christmas 1944, I was presented with a gift of so-called "premium coupons." These were issued by the construction firm to which we were practically sold as slaves: the firm paid the camp authorities a fixed price per day, per prisoner. The coupons cost the firm fifty pfennigs each and could be exchanged for six cigarettes, often weeks later, although they sometimes lost their validity. I became the proud owner of a token worth twelve cigarettes. But more important, the cigarettes could be exchanged for twelve soups, and twelve soups were often a very real respite from starvation.

The privilege of actually smoking cigarettes was reserved for the Capo, who had his assured quota of weekly coupons; or possibly for a prisoner who worked as a foreman in a warehouse or workshop and received a few cigarettes in exchange for doing dangerous jobs. The only exceptions to this were those who had lost the will to live and wanted to "enjoy" their last days. Thus, when we saw a comrade smoking his own cigarettes, we knew he had given up faith in his strength to carry on, and, once lost, the will to live seldom returned.

When one examines the vast amount of material which has been amassed as the result of many prisoners' observations and experiences, three phases of the inmate's mental reactions to camp life become apparent: the period following his admission; the period when he is well entrenched in camp routine; and the period following his release and liberation.

The symptom that characterizes the first phase is shock. Under certain conditions shock may even precede the prisoner's formal admission to the camp. I shall give as an example the circumstances of my own admission.

Fifteen hundred persons had been traveling by train for several days and nights: there were eighty people in each coach. All had to lie on top of their luggage, the few remnants of their personal possessions. The carriages were so full that only the top parts of the windows were free to let in the grey of dawn. Everyone expected the train to head for some munitions factory, in which we would be employed as forced labor. We did not know whether we were still in Silesia or already in Poland. The engine's whistle had an uncanny sound, like a cry for help sent out in commiseration for the unhappy load which it was destined to lead into perdition. Then the train shunted, obviously nearing a main station. Suddenly a cry broke from the ranks of the anxious passengers, "There is a sign, Auschwitz!" Everyone's heart missed a beat at that moment. Auschwitz—the very name stood for all that was horrible: gas chambers, crematoriums, massacres. Slowly, almost hesitatingly, the train moved on as if it wanted to spare its passengers the dreadful realization as long as possible: Auschwitz!

With the progressive dawn, the outlines of an immense camp became visible: long stretches of several rows of barbed wire fences; watch towers; search lights; and long columns of ragged human figures, grey in the greyness of dawn, trekking along the straight desolate roads, to what destination we did not know. There were isolated shouts and whistles of command. We did not know their meaning. My imagination led me to see gallows with people dangling on them. I was horrified, but this was just as well, because step by step we had to become accustomed to a terrible and immense horror.

Eventually we moved into the station. The initial silence was interrupted by shouted commands. We were to hear those rough, shrill tones from then on, over and

over again in all the camps. Their sound was almost like
the last cry of a victim, and yet there was a difference. It
had a rasping hoarseness, as if it came from the throat of
a man who had to keep shouting like that, a man who was
being murdered again and again. The carriage doors were
flung open and a small detachment of prisoners stormed
inside. They wore striped uniforms, their heads were
shaved, but they looked well fed. They spoke in every
possible European tongue, and all with a certain amount
of humor, which sounded grotesque under the circumstances. Like a drowning man clutching a straw, my in-
born optimism (which has often controlled my feelings
even in the most desperate situations) clung to this
thought: These prisoners look quite well, they seem to be
in good spirits and even laugh. Who knows? I might manage to share their favorable position.

   In psychiatry there is a certain condition known as
"delusion of reprieve." The condemned man, immediately
before his execution, gets the illusion that he might be reprieved at the very last minute. We, too, clung to shreds
of hope and believed to the last moment that it would not
be so bad. Just the sight of the red cheeks and round faces
of those prisoners was a great encouragement. Little did
we know then that they formed a specially chosen elite,
who for years had been the receiving squad for new transports as they rolled into the station day after day. They
took charge of the new arrivals and their luggage, including scarce items and smuggled jewelry. Auschwitz must
have been a strange spot in this Europe of the last years of
the war. There must have been unique treasures of gold
and silver, platinum and diamonds, not only in the huge
storehouses but also in the hands of the SS.

Fifteen hundred captives were cooped up in a shed built to accommodate probably two hundred at the most. We were cold and hungry and there was not enough room for everyone to squat on the bare ground, let alone to lie down. One five-ounce piece of bread was our only food in four days. Yet I heard the senior prisoners in charge of the shed bargain with one member of the receiving party about a tie-pin made of platinum and diamonds. Most of the profits would eventually be traded for liquor—schnapps. I do not remember any more just how many thousands of marks were needed to purchase the quantity of schnapps required for a "gay evening," but I do know that those long-term prisoners needed schnapps. Under such conditions, who could blame them for trying to dope themselves? There was another group of prisoners who got liquor supplied in almost unlimited quantities by the SS: these were the men who were employed in the gas chambers and crematoriums, and who knew very well that one day they would be relieved by a new shift of men, and that they would have to leave their enforced role of executioner and become victims themselves.

Nearly everyone in our transport lived under the illusion that he would be reprieved, that everything would yet be well. We did not realize the meaning behind the scene that was to follow presently. We were told to leave our luggage in the train and to fall into two lines—women on one side, men on the other—in order to file past a senior SS officer. Surprisingly enough, I had the courage to hide my haversack under my coat. My line filed past the officer, man by man. I realized that it would be dangerous if the officer spotted my bag. He would at least knock me down; I knew that from previous experience. Instinctively, I

straightened on approaching the officer, so that he would
not notice my heavy load. Then I was face to face with
him. He was a tall man who looked slim and fit in his
spotless uniform. What a contrast to us, who were untidy
and grimy after our long journey! He had assumed an attitude of careless ease, supporting his right elbow with his
left hand. His right hand was lifted, and with the fore-
finger of that hand he pointed very leisurely to the right
or to the left. None of us had the slightest idea of the
sinister meaning behind that little movement of a man's
finger, pointing now to the right and now to the left, but
far more frequently to the left.

It was my turn. Somebody whispered to me that to
be sent to the right side would mean work, the way to the
left being for the sick and those incapable of work, who
would be sent to a special camp. I just waited for things
to take their course, the first of many such times to come.
My haversack weighed me down a bit to the left, but I
made an effort to walk upright. The SS man looked me
over, appeared to hesitate, then put both his hands on my
shoulders. I tried very hard to look smart, and he turned
my shoulders very slowly until I faced right, and I moved
over to that side.

The significance of the finger game was explained to
us in the evening. It was the first selection, the first ver-
dict made on our existence or non-existence. For the great
majority of our transport, about 90 per cent, it meant
death. Their sentence was carried out within the next few
hours. Those who were sent to the left were marched from
the station straight to the crematorium. This building, as
I was told by someone who worked there, had the word
"bath" written over its doors in several European lan-

guages. On entering, each prisoner was handed a piece of soap, and then——but mercifully I do not need to describe the events which followed. Many accounts have been written about this horror.

We who were saved, the minority of our transport, found out the truth in the evening. I inquired from prisoners who had been there for some time where my colleague and friend P——had been sent.

"Was he sent to the left side?"

"Yes," I replied.

"Then you can see him there," I was told.

"Where?" A hand pointed to the chimney a few hundred yards off, which was sending a column of flame up into the grey sky of Poland. It dissolved into a sinister cloud of smoke.

"That's where your friend is, floating up to Heaven," was the answer. But I still did not understand until the truth was explained to me in plain words.

But I am telling things out of their turn. From a psychological point of view, we had a long, long way in front of us from the break of that dawn at the station until our first night's rest at the camp.

Escorted by SS guards with loaded guns, we were made to run from the station, past electrically charged barbed wire, through the camp, to the cleansing station; for those of us who had passed the first selection, this was a real bath. Again our illusion of reprieve found confirmation. The SS men seemed almost charming. Soon we found out their reason. They were nice to us as long as they saw watches on our wrists and could persuade us in well-meaning tones to hand them over. Would we not have to hand over all our possessions anyway, and why should not that relatively nice person have the watch? Maybe one day he would do one a good turn.

We waited in a shed which seemed to be the ante-room to the disinfecting chamber. SS men appeared and spread out blankets into which we had to throw all our possessions, all our watches and jewelry. There were still naïve prisoners among us who asked, to the amusement of the more seasoned ones who were there as helpers, if they could not keep a wedding ring, a medal or a good-luck piece. No one could yet grasp the fact that everything would be taken away.

I tried to take one of the old prisoners into my confidence. Approaching him furtively, I pointed to the roll of paper in the inner pocket of my coat and said, "Look, this is the manuscript of a scientific book. I know what you will say; that I should be grateful to escape with my life, that that should be all I can expect of fate. But I cannot help myself. I must keep this manuscript at all costs; it contains my life's work. Do you understand that?"

Yes, he was beginning to understand. A grin spread slowly over his face, first piteous, then more amused, mocking, insulting, until he bellowed one word at me in answer to my question, a word that was ever present in the vocabulary of the camp inmates: "Shit!" At that moment I saw the plain truth and did what marked the culminating point of the first phase of my psychological reaction: I struck out my whole former life.

Suddenly there was a stir among my fellow travelers, who had been standing about with pale, frightened faces, helplessly debating. Again we heard the hoarsely shouted commands. We were driven with blows into the immediate anteroom of the bath. There we assembled around an

SS man who waited until we had all arrived. Then he said, "I will give you two minutes, and I shall time you by my watch. In these two minutes you will get fully undressed and drop everything on the floor where you are standing. You will take nothing with you except your shoes, your belt or suspenders, and possibly a truss. I am starting to count—now!"

With unthinkable haste, people tore off their clothes. As the time grew shorter, they became increasingly nervous and pulled clumsily at their underwear, belts and shoelaces. Then we heard the first sounds of whipping; leather straps beating down on naked bodies.

Next we were herded into another room to be shaved: not only our heads were shorn, but not a hair was left on our entire bodies. Then on to the showers, where we lined up again. We hardly recognized each other; but with great relief some people noted that real water dripped from the sprays.

While we were waiting for the shower, our nakedness was brought home to us: we really had nothing now except our bare bodies—even minus hair; all we possessed, literally, was our naked existence. What else remained for us as a material link with our former lives? For me there were my glasses and my belt; the latter I had to exchange later on for a piece of bread. There was an extra bit of excitement in store for the owners of trusses. In the evening the senior prisoner in charge of our hut welcomed us with a speech in which he gave us his word of honor that he would hang, personally, "from that beam"—he pointed to it—any person who had sewn money or precious stones into his truss. Proudly he explained that as a senior inhabitant the camp laws entitled him to do so.

Where our shoes were concerned, matters were not so simple. Although we were supposed to keep them, those who had fairly decent pairs had to give them up after all and were given in exchange shoes that did not fit. In for real trouble were those prisoners who had followed the apparently well-meant advice (given in the anteroom) of the senior prisoners and had shortened their jackboots by cutting the tops off, then smearing soap on the cut edges to hide the sabotage. The SS men seemed to have waited for just that. All suspected of this crime had to go into a small adjoining room. After a time we again heard the lashings of the strap, and the screams of tortured men. This time it lasted for quite a while.

Thus the illusions some of us still held were destroyed one by one, and then, quite unexpectedly, most of us were overcome by a grim sense of humor. We knew that we had nothing to lose except our so ridiculously naked lives. When the showers started to run, we all tried very hard to make fun, both about ourselves and about each other. After all, real water did flow from the sprays!

Apart from that strange kind of humor, another sensation seized us: curiosity. I have experienced this kind of curiosity before, as a fundamental reaction toward certain strange circumstances. When my life was once endangered by a climbing accident, I felt only one sensation at the critical moment: curiosity, curiosity as to whether I should come out of it alive or with a fractured skull or some other injuries.

Cold curiosity predominated even in Auschwitz, somehow detaching the mind from its surroundings, which came to be regarded with a kind of objectivity. At that time one cultivated this state of mind as a means of pro-

tection. We were anxious to know what would happen
next; and what would be the consequence, for example,
of our standing in the open air, in the chill of late autumn,
stark naked, and still wet from the showers. In the next
few days our curiosity evolved into surprise; surprise that
we did not catch cold.

There were many similar surprises in store for new
arrivals. The medical men among us learned first of all:
"Textbooks tell lies!" Somewhere it is said that man cannot exist without sleep for more than a stated number of
hours. Quite wrong! I had been convinced that there were
certain things I just could not do: I could not sleep without this or I could not live with that or the other. The first
night in Auschwitz we slept in beds which were constructed in tiers. On each tier (measuring about six-and-
a-half to eight feet) slept nine men, directly on the
boards. Two blankets were shared by each nine men. We
could, of course, lie only on our sides, crowded and huddled against each other, which had some advantages because of the bitter cold. Though it was forbidden to take
shoes up to the bunks, some people did use them secretly
as pillows in spite of the fact that they were caked with
mud. Otherwise one's head had to rest on the crook of an
almost dislocated arm. And yet sleep came and brought
oblivion and relief from pain for a few hours.

I would like to mention a few similar surprises on how
much we could endure: we were unable to clean our teeth,
and yet, in spite of that and a severe vitamin deficiency,
we had healthier gums than ever before. We had to wear
the same shirts for half a year, until they had lost all ap-
pearance of being shirts. For days we were unable to wash,
even partially, because of frozen water-pipes, and yet the

sores and abrasions on hands which were dirty from work in the soil did not suppurate (that is, unless there was frostbite). Or for instance, a light sleeper, who used to be disturbed by the slightest noise in the next room, now found himself lying pressed against a comrade who snored loudly a few inches from his ear and yet slept quite soundly through the noise.

If someone now asked of us the truth of Dostoevski's statement that flatly defines man as a being who can get used to anything, we would reply, "Yes, a man can get used to anything, but do not ask us how." But our psychological investigations have not taken us that far yet; neither had we prisoners reached that point. We were still in the first phase of our psychological reactions.

The thought of suicide was entertained by nearly everyone, if only for a brief time. It was born of the hopelessness of the situation, the constant danger of death looming over us daily and hourly, and the closeness of the deaths suffered by many of the others. From personal convictions which will be mentioned later, I made myself a firm promise, on my first evening in camp, that I would not "run into the wire." This was a phrase used in camp to describe the most popular method of suicide—touching the electrically charged barbed-wire fence. It was not entirely difficult for me to make this decision. There was little point in committing suicide, since, for the average inmate, life expectation, calculating objectively and counting all likely chances, was very poor. He could not with any assurance expect to be among the small percentage of men who survived all the selections. The prisoner of Auschwitz, in the first phase of shock, did not fear death. Even the gas chambers lost their horrors for him after the first few days—after all, they spared him the act of committing suicide.

Friends whom I have met later have told me that I was not one of those whom the shock of admission greatly depressed. I only smiled, and quite sincerely, when the following episode occurred the morning after our first night in Auschwitz. In spite of strict orders not to leave our "blocks," a colleague of mine, who had arrived in Auschwitz several weeks previously, smuggled himself into our hut. He wanted to calm and comfort us and tell us a few things. He had become so thin that at first we did not recognize him. With a show of good humor and a Devil-may-care attitude he gave us a few hurried tips: "Don't be afraid! Don't fear the selections! Dr. M——— (the SS medical chief) has a soft spot for doctors." (This was wrong; my friend's kindly words were misleading. One prisoner, the doctor of a block of huts and a man of some sixty years, told me how he had entreated Dr. M——— to let off his son, who was destined for gas. Dr. M——— coldly refused.)

"But one thing I beg of you"; he continued, "shave daily, if at all possible, even if you have to use a piece of glass to do it . . . even if you have to give your last piece of bread for it. You will look younger and the scraping will make your cheeks look ruddier. If you want to stay alive, there is only one way: look fit for work. If you even limp, because, let us say, you have a small blister on your heel, and an SS man spots this, he will wave you aside and the next day you are sure to be gassed. Do you know what we mean by a 'Moslem'? A man who looks miserable, down and out, sick and emaciated, and who cannot manage hard physical labor any longer . . . that is a 'Moslem.' Sooner or later, usually sooner, every 'Moslem' goes to the gas chambers. Therefore, remember: shave, stand and walk smartly; then you need not be afraid of gas. All of you standing here, even if you have only been here twenty-four hours, you need not fear gas, except perhaps you." And then he pointed to me and said, "I hope you don't mind my telling you frankly." To the others he repeated, "Of all of you he is the only one who must fear the next selection. So, don't worry!"

And I smiled. I am now convinced that anyone in my place on that day would have done the same.

I think it was Lessing who once said, "There are things which must cause you to lose your reason or you have none to lose." An abnormal reaction to an abnormal situation is normal behavior. Even we psychiatrists expect the reactions of a man to an abnormal situation, such as being committed to an asylum, to be abnormal in proportion to the degree of his normality. The reaction of a man to his admission to a concentration camp also represents an abnormal state of mind, but judged objectively it is a normal and, as will be shown later, typical reaction to the given circumstances. These reactions, as I have described them, began to change in a few days. The prisoner passed from the first to the second phase; the phase of relative apathy, in which he achieved a kind of emotional death.

Apart from the already described reactions, the newly arrived prisoner experienced the tortures of other most painful emotions, all of which he tried to deaden. First of all, there was his boundless longing for his home and his family. This often could become so acute that he felt himself consumed by longing. Then there was disgust; disgust with all the ugliness which surrounded him, even in its mere external forms.

Most of the prisoners were given a uniform of rags which would have made a scarecrow elegant by comparison. Between the huts in the camp lay pure filth, and the more one worked to clear it away, the more one had to come in contact with it. It was a favorite practice to detail a new arrival to a work group whose job was to clean the latrines and remove the sewage. If, as usually happened, some of the excrement splashed into his face during its transport over bumpy fields, any sign of disgust by the prisoner or any attempt to wipe off the filth would only be punished with a blow from a Capo. And thus the mortification of normal reactions was hastened.

At first the prisoner looked away if he saw the punishment parades of another group; he could not bear to see fellow prisoners march up and down for hours in the mire, their movements directed by blows. Days or weeks later things changed. Early in the morning, when it was still dark, the prisoner stood in front of the gate with his detachment, ready to march. He heard a scream and saw how a comrade was knocked down, pulled to his feet again, and knocked down once more—and why? He was feverish but had reported to sick-bay at an improper time. He was being punished for this irregular attempt to be relieved of his duties.

But the prisoner who had passed into the second stage of his psychological reactions did not avert his eyes any more. By then his feelings were blunted, and he watched unmoved. Another example: he found himself waiting at sick-bay, hoping to be granted two days of light work in-side the camp because of injuries or perhaps edema or fever. He stood unmoved while a twelve-year-old boy was carried in who had been forced to stand at attention for hours in the snow or to work outside with bare feet because there were no shoes for him in the camp. His toes had be-come frostbitten, and the doctor on duty picked off the black gangrenous stumps with tweezers, one by one. Dis-gust, horror and pity are emotions that our spectator could not really feel any more. The sufferers, the dying and the dead, became such commonplace sights to him after a few weeks of camp life that they could not move him any more.

I spent some time in a hut for typhus patients who ran very high temperatures and were often delirious, many of them moribund. After one of them had just died, I watched without any emotional upset the scene that fol-lowed, which was repeated over and over again with each death. One by one the prisoners approached the still warm body. One grabbed the remains of a messy meal of potatoes; another decided that the corpse's wooden shoes were an improvement on his own, and exchanged them. A third man did the same with the dead man's coat, and another was glad to be able to secure some—just imagine!—genuine string.

All this I watched with unconcern. Eventually I asked the "nurse" to remove the body. When he decided to do so, he took the corpse by its legs, allowing it to drop into the small corridor between the two rows of boards which were the beds for the fifty typhus patients, and dragged it across the bumpy earthen floor toward the door. The two steps which led up into the open air always constituted a problem for us, since we were exhausted from a chronic lack of food. After a few months' stay in the camp we could not walk up those steps, which were each about six inches high, without putting our hands on the door jambs to pull ourselves up.

The man with the corpse approached the steps. Wearily he dragged himself up. Then the body: first the feet, then the trunk, and finally—with an uncanny rattling noise—the head of the corpse bumped up the two steps.

My place was on the opposite side of the hut, next to the small, sole window, which was built near the floor. While my cold hands clasped a bowl of hot soup from which I sipped greedily, I happened to look out the window. The corpse which had just been removed stared in at me with glazed eyes. Two hours before I had spoken to that man. Now I continued sipping my soup.

If my lack of emotion had not surprised me from the standpoint of professional interest, I would not remember this incident now, because there was so little feeling involved in it.

Apathy, the blunting of the emotions and the feeling that one could not care any more, were the symptoms arising during the second stage of the prisoner's psychological reactions, and which eventually made him insensitive to daily and hourly beatings. By means of this insensibility the prisoner soon surrounded himself with a very necessary protective shell.

Beatings occurred on the slightest provocation, sometimes for no reason at all. For example, bread was rationed
out at our work site and we had to line up for it. Once,
the man behind me stood off a little to one side and that
lack of symmetry displeased the SS guard. I did not know
what was going on in the line behind me, nor in the mind
of the SS guard, but suddenly I received two sharp blows
on my head. Only then did I spot the guard at my side who
was using his stick. At such a moment it is not the physical pain which hurts the most (and this applies to adults
as much as to punished children); it is the mental agony
caused by the injustice, the unreasonableness of it all.

Strangely enough, a blow which does not even find
its mark can, under certain circumstances, hurt more than
one that finds its mark. Once I was standing on a railway
track in a snowstorm. In spite of the weather our party
had to keep on working. I worked quite hard at mending
the track with gravel, since that was the only way to keep
warm. For only one moment I paused to get my breath
and to lean on my shovel. Unfortunately the guard turned
around just then and thought I was loafing. The pain he
caused me was not from any insults or any blows. That
guard did not think it worth his while to say anything,
not even a swear word, to the ragged, emaciated figure
standing before him, which probably reminded him only
vaguely of a human form. Instead, he playfully picked
up a stone and threw it at me. That, to me, seemed the
way to attract the attention of a beast, to call a domestic
animal back to its job, a creature with which you have so
little in common that you do not even punish it.

The most painful part of beatings is the insult which

they imply. At one time we had to carry some long, heavy girders over icy tracks. If one man slipped, he endangered not only himself but all the others who carried the same girder. An old friend of mine had a congenitally dislocated hip. He was glad to be capable of working in spite of it, since the physically disabled were almost certainly sent to death when a selection took place. He limped over the track with an especially heavy girder, and seemed about to fall and drag the others with him. As yet, I was not carrying a girder so I jumped to his assistance without stopping to think. I was immediately hit on the back, rudely reprimanded and ordered to return to my place. A few minutes previously the same guard who struck me had told us deprecatingly that we "pigs" lacked the spirit of comradeship.

Another time, in a forest, with the temperature at 2°F, we began to dig up the topsoil, which was frozen hard, in order to lay water pipes. By then I had grown rather weak physically. Along came a foreman with chubby rosy cheeks. His face definitely reminded me of a pig's head. I noticed that he wore lovely warm gloves in that bitter cold. For a time he watched me silently. I felt that trouble was brewing, for in front of me lay the mound of earth which showed exactly how much I had dug.

Then he began: "You pig, I have been watching you the whole time! I'll teach you to work, yet! Wait till you dig dirt with your teeth—you'll die like an animal! In two days I'll finish you off! You've never done a stroke of work in your life. What were you, swine? A businessman?"

I was past caring. But I had to take his threat of killing me seriously, so I straightened up and looked him directly in the eye. "I was a doctor—a specialist."

"What? A doctor? I bet you got a lot of money out of people."

"As it happens, I did most of my work for no money at all, in clinics for the poor." But, now, I had said too much. He threw himself on me and knocked me down, shouting like a madman. I can no longer remember what he shouted.

I want to show with this apparently trivial story that there are moments when indignation can rouse even a seemingly hardened prisoner—indignation not about cruelty or pain, but about the insult connected with it. That time blood rushed to my head because I had to listen to a man judge my life who had so little idea of it, a man (I must confess: the following remark, which I made to my fellow-prisoners after the scene, afforded me childish relief) "who looked so vulgar and brutal that the nurse in the out-patient ward in my hospital would not even have admitted him to the waiting room."

Fortunately the Capo in my working party was obligated to me; he had taken a liking to me because I listened to his love stories and matrimonial troubles, which he poured out during the long marches to our work site. I had made an impression on him with my diagnosis of his character and with my psychotherapeutic advice. After that he was grateful, and this had already been of value to me. On several previous occasions he had reserved a place for me next to him in one of the first five rows of our detachment, which usually consisted of two hundred and eighty men. That favor was important. We had to line up early in the morning while it was still dark. Everybody was afraid of being late and of having to stand in the back rows. If men were required for an unpleasant and disliked job, the senior Capo appeared and usually collected the men he needed from the back rows. These men had to march away to another, especially dreaded kind of work under the command of strange guards. Occasionally the senior Capo chose men from the first five rows, just to catch those who tried to be clever. All protests and entreaties were silenced by a few well-aimed kicks, and the chosen victims were chased to the meeting place with shouts and blows.

However, as long as my Capo felt the need of pouring out his heart, this could not happen to me. I had a guaranteed place of honor next to him. But there was another advantage, too. Like nearly all the camp inmates I was suffering from edema. My legs were so swollen and the skin on them so tightly stretched that I could scarcely bend my knees. I had to leave my shoes unlaced in order to make them fit my swollen feet. There would not have been space for socks even if I had had any. So my partly bare feet were always wet and my shoes always full of snow. This, of course, caused frostbite and chilblains. Every single step became real torture. Clumps of ice formed on our shoes during our marches over snow-covered fields. Over and again men slipped and those following behind stumbled on top of them. Then the column would stop for a moment, but not for long. One of the guards soon took action and worked over the men with the butt of his rifle to make them get up quickly. The more to the front of the column you were, the less often you were disturbed by having to stop and then to make up for lost time by running on your painful feet. I was very happy to be the personally appointed physician to His Honor the Capo, and to march in the first row at an even pace.

As an additional payment for my services, I could be sure that as long as soup was being dealt out at lunchtime at our work site, he would, when my turn came, dip the ladle right to the bottom of the vat and fish out a few peas. This Capo, a former army officer, even had the courage to whisper to the foreman, whom I had quarreled with, that he knew me to be an unusually good worker. That didn't help matters, but he nevertheless managed to save my life (one of the many times it was to be saved). The day after the episode with the foreman he smuggled me into another work party.

There were foremen who felt sorry for us and who did their best to ease our situation, at least at the building site. But even they kept on reminding us that an ordinary laborer did several times as much work as we did, and in a shorter time. But they did see reason if they were told that a normal workman did not live on 10½ ounces of bread (theoretically—actually we often had less) and 1¾ pints of thin soup per day; that a normal laborer did not live under the mental stress we had to submit to, not having news of our families, who had either been sent to another camp or gassed right away; that a normal workman was not threatened by death continuously, daily and hourly. I even allowed myself to say once to a kindly foreman, "If you could learn from me how to do a brain operation in as short a time as I am learning this road work from you, I would have great respect for you." And he grinned.

Apathy, the main symptom of the second phase, was a necessary mechanism of self-defense. Reality dimmed, and all efforts and all emotions were centered on one task: preserving one's own life and that of the other fellow. It was typical to hear the prisoners, while they were being herded back to camp from their work sites in the evening, sigh with relief and say, "Well, another day is over."

It can be readily understood that such a state of strain, coupled with the constant necessity of concentrating on the task of staying alive, forced the prisoner's inner life down to a primitive level. Several of my colleagues in camp who were trained in psychoanalysis often spoke of a "regression" in the camp inmate—a retreat to a more primitive form of mental life. His wishes and desires became obvious in his dreams.

What did the prisoner dream about most frequently? Of bread, cake, cigarettes, and nice warm baths. The lack of having these simple desires satisfied led him to seek wish-fulfillment in dreams. Whether these dreams did any good is another matter; the dreamer had to wake from them to the reality of camp life, and to the terrible contrast between that and his dream illusions.

I shall never forget how I was roused one night by the groans of a fellow prisoner, who threw himself about in his sleep, obviously having a horrible nightmare. Since I had always been especially sorry for people who suffered from fearful dreams or deliria, I wanted to wake the

poor man. Suddenly I drew back the hand which was
ready to shake him, frightened at the thing I was about
to do. At that moment I became intensely conscious of the
fact that no dream, no matter how horrible, could be as
bad as the reality of the camp which surrounded us, and
to which I was about to recall him.

Because of the high degree of undernourishment
which the prisoners suffered, it was natural that the desire
for food was the major primitive instinct around which
mental life centered. Let us observe the majority of prisoners when they happened to work near each other and
were, for once, not closely watched. They would immediately start discussing food. One fellow would ask another working next to him in the ditch what his favorite
dishes were. Then they would exchange recipes and plan
the menu for the day when they would have a reunion—
the day in a distant future when they would be liberated
and returned home. They would go on and on, picturing
it all in detail, until suddenly a warning was passed down
the trench, usually in the form of a special password or
number: "The guard is coming."

I always regarded the discussions about food as dangerous. Is it not wrong to provoke the organism with such
detailed and affective pictures of delicacies when it has
somehow managed to adapt itself to extremely small ra-
tions and low calories? Though it may afford momen-
tary psychological relief, it is an illusion which physio-
logically, surely, must not be without danger.

During the later part of our imprisonment, the daily
ration consisted of very watery soup given out once daily,

and the usual small bread ration. In addition to that, there was the so-called "extra allowance," consisting of three-fourths of an ounce of margarine, or of a slice of poor quality sausage, or of a little piece of cheese, or a bit of synthetic honey, or a spoonful of watery jam, varying daily. In calories, this diet was absolutely inadequate, especially taking into consideration our heavy manual work and our constant exposure to the cold in inadequate clothing. The sick who were "under special care"—that is, those who were allowed to lie in the huts instead of leaving the camp for work—were even worse off.

When the last layers of subcutaneous fat had vanished, and we looked like skeletons disguised with skin and rags, we could watch our bodies beginning to devour themselves. The organism digested its own protein, and the muscles disappeared. Then the body had no powers of resistance left. One after another the members of the little community in our hut died. Each of us could calculate with fair accuracy whose turn would be next, and when his own would come. After many observations we knew the symptoms well, which made the correctness of our prognoses quite certain. "He won't last long," or, "This is the next one," we whispered to each other, and when, during our daily search for lice, we saw our own naked bodies in the evening, we thought alike: This body here, my body, is really a corpse already. What has become of me? I am but a small portion of a great mass of human flesh . . . of a mass behind barbed wire, crowded into a few earthen huts; a mass of which daily a certain portion begins to rot because it has become lifeless.

I mentioned above how unavoidable were the thoughts about food and favorite dishes which forced

themselves into the consciousness of the prisoner, whenever he had a moment to spare. Perhaps it can be understood, then, that even the strongest of us was longing for
the time when he would have fairly good food again, not
for the sake of good food itself, but for the sake of knowing that the sub-human existence, which had made us
unable to think of anything other than food, would at
last cease.

Those who have not gone through a similar experience can hardly conceive of the soul-destroying mental
conflict and clashes of will power which a famished man
experiences. They can hardly grasp what it means to stand
digging in a trench, listening only for the siren to an-
nounce 9:30 or 10:00 A.M.—the half-hour lunch interval
—when bread would be rationed out (as long as it was
still available); repeatedly asking the foreman—if he
wasn't a disagreeable fellow—what the time was; and
tenderly touching a piece of bread in one's coat pocket,
first stroking it with frozen gloveless fingers, then break-
ing off a crumb and putting it in one's mouth and finally,
with the last bit of will power, pocketing it again, having
promised oneself that morning to hold out till afternoon.

We could hold endless debates on the sense or non-
sense of certain methods of dealing with the small bread
ration, which was given out only once daily during the
latter part of our confinement. There were two schools of
thought. One was in favor of eating up the ration immediately. This had the twofold advantage of satisfying
the worst hunger pangs for a very short time at least once
a day and of safeguarding against possible theft or loss
of the ration. The second group, which held with dividing

the ration up, used different arguments. I finally joined their ranks.

The most ghastly moment of the twenty-four hours of camp life was the awakening, when, at a still nocturnal hour, the three shrill blows of a whistle tore us pitilessly from our exhausted sleep and from the longings in our dreams. We then began the tussle with our wet shoes, into which we could scarcely force our feet, which were sore and swollen with edema. And there were the usual moans and groans about petty troubles, such as the snapping of wires which replaced shoelaces. One morning I heard someone, whom I knew to be brave and dignified, cry like a child because he finally had to go to the snowy marching grounds in his bare feet, as his shoes were too shrunken for him to wear. In those ghastly minutes, I found a little bit of comfort; a small piece of bread which I drew out of my pocket and munched with absorbed delight.

Undernourishment, besides being the cause of the general preoccupation with food, probably also explains the fact that the sexual urge was generally absent. Apart from the initial effects of shock, this appears to be the only explanation of a phenomenon which a psychologist was bound to observe in those all-male camps: that, as opposed to all other strictly male establishments—such as army barracks—there was little sexual perversion. Even in his dreams the prisoner did not seem to concern himself with sex, although his frustrated emotions and his finer, higher feelings did find definite expression in them.

With the majority of the prisoners, the primitive life and the effort of having to concentrate on just saving one's skin led to a total disregard of anything not serving that purpose, and explained the prisoners' complete lack of sentiment. This was brought home to me on my transfer from Auschwitz to a camp affiliated with Dachau. The train which carried us—about 2,000 prisoners—passed through Vienna. At about midnight we passed one of the Viennese railway stations. The track was going to lead us past the street where I was born, past the house where I had lived many years of my life, in fact, until I was taken prisoner.

There were fifty of us in the prison car, which had two small, barred peepholes. There was only enough room for one group to squat on the floor, while the others, who had to stand up for hours, crowded round the peepholes. Standing on tiptoe and looking past the others' heads through the bars of the window, I caught an eerie glimpse of my native town. We all felt more dead than alive, since we thought that our transport was heading for the camp at Mauthausen and that we had only one or two weeks to live. I had a distinct feeling that I saw the streets, the squares and the houses of my childhood with the eyes of a dead man who had come back from another world and was looking down on a ghostly city.

After hours of delay the train left the station. And there was the street—my street! The young lads who had a number of years of camp life behind them and for whom such a journey was a great event stared attentively through the peephole. I began to beg them, to entreat them, to let me stand in front for one moment only. I tried to explain how much a look through that window meant to me just

then. My request was refused with rudeness and cyni-
cism: "You lived here all those years? Well, then you have
seen quite enough already!"

In general there was also a "cultural hibernation" in
the camp. There were two exceptions to this: politics
and religion. Politics were talked about everywhere in
camp, almost continuously; the discussions were based
chiefly on rumors, which were snapped up and passed
around avidly. The rumors about the military situation
were usually contradictory. They followed one another
rapidly and succeeded only in making a contribution to
the war of nerves that was waged in the minds of all the
prisoners. Many times, hopes for a speedy end to the war,
which had been fanned by optimistic rumors, were disappointed. Some men lost all hope, but it was the incor-
rigible optimists who were the most irritating companions.

The religious interest of the prisoners, as far and as
soon as it developed, was the most sincere imaginable. The
depth and vigor of religious belief often surprised and
moved a new arrival. Most impressive in this connection
were improvised prayers or services in the corner of a hut,
or in the darkness of the locked cattle truck in which we
were brought back from a distant work site, tired, hungry and frozen in our ragged clothing.

In the winter and spring of 1945 there was an outbreak of typhus which infected nearly all the prisoners.
The mortality was great among the weak, who had to
keep on with their hard work as long as they possibly
could. The quarters for the sick were most inadequate,
there were practically no medicines or attendants. Some

of the symptoms of the disease were extremely disagreeable: an irrepressible aversion to even a scrap of food (which was an additional danger to life) and terrible attacks of delirium. The worst case of delirium was suffered by a friend of mine who thought that he was dying and wanted to pray. In his delirium he could not find the words to do so. To avoid these attacks of delirium, I tried, as did many of the others, to keep awake for most of the night. For hours I composed speeches in my mind. Eventually I began to reconstruct the manuscript which I had lost in the disinfection chamber of Auschwitz, and scribbled the key words in shorthand on tiny scraps of paper.

Occasionally a scientific debate developed in camp. Once I witnessed something I had never seen, even in my normal life, although it lay somewhat near my own professional interests: a spiritualistic seance. I had been invited to attend by the camp's chief doctor (also a prisoner), who knew that I was a specialist in psychiatry. The meeting took place in his small, private room in the sick quarters. A small circle had gathered, among them, quite illegally, the warrant officer from the sanitation squad.

One man began to invoke the spirits with a kind of prayer. The camp's clerk sat in front of a blank sheet of paper, without any conscious intention of writing. During the next ten minutes (after which time the seance was terminated because of the medium's failure to conjure the spirits to appear) his pencil slowly drew lines across the paper, forming quite legibly "VAE V." It was asserted that the clerk had never learned Latin and that he had never before heard the words *"vae victis"*—woe to the vanquished. In my opinion he must have heard them once in his life, without recollecting them, and they must have been available to the "spirit" (the spirit of his subconscious mind) at that time, a few months before our liberation and the end of the war.

In spite of all the enforced physical and mental primitiveness of the life in a concentration camp, it was possible for spiritual life to deepen. Sensitive people who were used to a rich intellectual life may have suffered much pain (they were often of a delicate constitution), but the damage to their inner selves was less. They were able to retreat from their terrible surroundings to a life of inner riches and spiritual freedom. Only in this way can one explain the apparent paradox that some prisoners of a less hardy make-up often seemed to survive camp life better than did those of a robust nature. In order to make myself clear, I am forced to fall back on personal experience. Let me tell what happened on those early mornings when we had to march to our work site.

There were shouted commands: "Detachment, forward march! Left-2-3-4! Left-2-3-4! Left-2-3-4! Left-2-3-4! First man about, left and left and left and left! Caps off!" These words sound in my ears even now. At the order "Caps off!" we passed the gate of the camp, and searchlights were trained upon us. Whoever did not march smartly got a kick. And worse off was the man who, because of the cold, had pulled his cap back over his ears before permission was given.

We stumbled on in the darkness, over big stones and through large puddles, along the one road leading from the camp. The accompanying guards kept shouting at us and driving us with the butts of their rifles. Anyone with very sore feet supported himself on his neighbor's arm. Hardly a word was spoken; the icy wind did not encourage talk. Hiding his mouth behind his upturned collar, the man marching next to me whispered suddenly: "If our wives could see us now! I do hope they are better off in their camps and don't know what is happening to us."

That brought thoughts of my own wife to mind. And as we stumbled on for miles, slipping on icy spots, supporting each other time and again, dragging one another up and onward, nothing was said, but we both knew: each of us was thinking of his wife. Occasionally I looked at the sky, where the stars were fading and the pink light of the morning was beginning to spread behind a dark bank of clouds. But my mind clung to my wife's image, imagining it with an uncanny acuteness. I heard her answering me, saw her smile, her frank and encouraging look. Real or not, her look was then more luminous than the sun which was beginning to rise.

A thought transfixed me: for the first time in my life I saw the truth as it is set into song by so many poets, proclaimed as the final wisdom by so many thinkers. The truth—that love is the ultimate and the highest goal to which man can aspire. Then I grasped the meaning of the greatest secret that human poetry and human thought and belief have to impart: *The salvation of man is through love and in love.* I understood how a man who has nothing left in this world still may know bliss, be it only for a brief moment, in the contemplation of his beloved. In a position of utter desolation, when man cannot express himself in positive action, when his only achievement may consist in enduring his sufferings in the right way—an honorable way—in such a position man can, through loving contemplation of the image he carries of his beloved, achieve fulfillment. For the first time in my life I was able to understand the meaning of the words, "The angels are lost in perpetual contemplation of an infinite glory."

In front of me a man stumbled and those following him fell on top of him. The guard rushed over and used his whip on them all. Thus my thoughts were interrupted for a few minutes. But soon my soul found its way back from the prisoner's existence to another world, and I resumed talk with my loved one: I asked her questions, and she answered; she questioned me in return, and I answered.

"Stop!" We had arrived at our work site. Everybody rushed into the dark hut in the hope of getting a fairly decent tool. Each prisoner got a spade or a pickaxe.

"Can't you hurry up, you pigs?" Soon we had resumed the previous day's positions in the ditch. The frozen ground cracked under the point of the pickaxes, and sparks flew. The men were silent, their brains numb.

My mind still clung to the image of my wife. A thought crossed my mind: I didn't even know if she were still alive. I knew only one thing—which I have learned well by now: Love goes very far beyond the physical person of the beloved. It finds its deepest meaning in his spiritual being, his inner self. Whether or not he is actually present, whether or not he is still alive at all, ceases somehow to be of importance.

I did not know whether my wife was alive, and I had no means of finding out (during all my prison life there was no outgoing or incoming mail); but at that moment it ceased to matter. There was no need for me to know; nothing could touch the strength of my love, my thoughts, and the image of my beloved. Had I known

then that my wife was dead, I think that I would still have
given myself, undisturbed by that knowledge, to the contemplation of her image, and that my mental conversation with her would have been just as vivid and just as
satisfying. "Set me like a seal upon thy heart, love is as
strong as death."

This intensification of inner life helped the prisoner
find a refuge from the emptiness, desolation and spiritual
poverty of his existence, by letting him escape into the
past. When given free rein, his imagination played with
past events, often not important ones, but minor happen-
ings and trifling things. His nostalgic memory glorified
them and they assumed a strange character. Their world
and their existence seemed very distant and the spirit
reached out for them longingly: In my mind I took bus
rides, unlocked the front door of my apartment, answered
my telephone, switched on the electric lights. Our
thoughts often centered on such details, and these memories could move one to tears.

As the inner life of the prisoner tended to become
more intense, he also experienced the beauty of art and
nature as never before. Under their influence he sometimes even forgot his own frightful circumstances. If
someone had seen our faces on the journey from Auschwitz to a Bavarian camp as we beheld the mountains of
Salzburg with their summits glowing in the sunset,
through the little barred windows of the prison carriage,
he would never have believed that those were the faces of
men who had given up all hope of life and liberty. Despite
that factor—or maybe because of it—we were carried

away by nature's beauty, which we had missed for so long.

In camp, too, a man might draw the attention of a comrade working next to him to a nice view of the setting sun shining through the tall trees of the Bavarian woods (as in the famous water color by Dürer), the same woods in which we had built an enormous, hidden munitions plant. One evening, when we were already resting on the floor of our hut, dead tired, soup bowls in hand, a fellow prisoner rushed in and asked us to run out to the assembly grounds and see the wonderful sunset. Standing outside we saw sinister clouds glowing in the west and the whole sky alive with clouds of ever-changing shapes and colors, from steel blue to blood red. The desolate grey mud huts provided a sharp contrast, while the puddles on the muddy ground reflected the glowing sky. Then, after minutes of moving silence, one prisoner said to another, "How beautiful the world *could* be!"

Another time we were at work in a trench. The dawn was grey around us; grey was the sky above; grey the snow in the pale light of dawn; grey the rags in which my fellow prisoners were clad, and grey their faces. I was again conversing silently with my wife, or perhaps I was struggling to find the *reason* for my sufferings, my slow dying. In a last violent protest against the hopelessness of imminent death, I sensed my spirit piercing through the enveloping gloom. I felt it transcend that hopeless, meaningless world, and from somewhere I heard a victorious "Yes" in answer to my question of the existence of an ultimate purpose. At that moment a light was lit in a distant farmhouse, which stood on the horizon as if painted there, in the midst of the miserable grey of a dawning morning in Bavaria. *"Et lux in tenebris lucet"*—

and the light shineth in the darkness. For hours I stood hacking at the icy ground. The guard passed by, insulting me, and once again I communed with my beloved. More and more I felt that she was present, that she was with me; I had the feeling that I was able to touch her, able to stretch out my hand and grasp hers. The feeling was very strong: she was *there*. Then, at that very moment, a bird flew down silently and perched just in front of me, on the heap of soil which I had dug up from the ditch, and looked steadily at me.

Earlier, I mentioned art. Is there such a thing in a concentration camp? It rather depends on what one chooses to call art. A kind of cabaret was improvised from time to time. A hut was cleared temporarily, a few wooden benches were pushed or nailed together and a program was drawn up. In the evening those who had fairly good positions in camp—the Capos and the workers who did not have to leave camp on distant marches—assembled there. They came to have a few laughs or perhaps to cry a little; anyway, to forget. There were songs, poems, jokes, some with underlying satire regarding the camp. All were meant to help us forget, and they did help. The gatherings were so effective that a few ordinary prisoners went to see the cabaret in spite of their fatigue even though they missed their daily portion of food by going.

During the half-hour lunch interval when soup (which the contractors paid for and for which they did not spend much) was ladled out at our work site, we were allowed to assemble in an unfinished engine room. On entering, everyone got a ladleful of the watery soup.

While we sipped it greedily, a prisoner climbed onto a tub and sang Italian arias. We enjoyed the songs, and he was guaranteed a double helping of soup, straight "from the bottom"—that meant with peas!

Rewards were given in camp not only for entertainment, but also for applause. I, for example, could have found protection (how lucky I was never in need of it!) from the camp's most dreaded Capo, who for more than one good reason was known as "The Murderous Capo." This is how it happened. One evening I had the great honor of being invited again to the room where the spiritualistic seance had taken place. There were gathered the same intimate friends of the chief doctor and, most illegally, the warrant officer from the sanitation squad was again present. The Murderous Capo entered the room by chance, and he was asked to recite one of his poems, which had become famous (or infamous) in camp. He did not need to be asked twice and quickly produced a kind of diary from which he began to read samples of his art. I bit my lips till they hurt in order to keep from laughing at one of his love poems, and very likely that saved my life. Since I was also generous with my applause, my life might have been saved even had I been detailed to his working party to which I had previously been assigned for one day—a day that was quite enough for me. It was useful, anyway, to be known to The Murderous Capo from a favorable angle. So I applauded as hard as I could.

Generally speaking, of course, any pursuit of art in camp was somewhat grotesque. I would say that the real impression made by anything connected with art arose only from the ghostlike contrast between the performance and the background of desolate camp life. I shall never forget how I awoke from the deep sleep of exhaustion on my second night in Auschwitz—roused by music. The senior warden of the hut had some kind of celebration in his room, which was near the entrance of the hut. Tipsy voices bawled some hackneyed tunes. Suddenly there was a silence and into the night a violin sang a desperately sad tango, an unusual tune not spoiled by frequent playing. The violin wept and a part of me wept with it, for on that same day someone had a twenty-fourth birthday. That someone lay in another part of the Auschwitz camp, possibly only a few hundred or a thousand yards away, and yet completely out of reach. That someone was my wife.

To discover that there was any semblance of art in a concentration camp must be surprise enough for an outsider, but he may be even more astonished to hear that one could find a sense of humor there as well; of course, only the faint trace of one, and then only for a few seconds or minutes. Humor was another of the soul's weapons in the fight for self-preservation. It is well known that humor, more than anything else in the human make-up, can afford an aloofness and an ability to rise above any situation, even if only for a few seconds. I practically trained a friend of mine who worked next to me on the building site to develop a sense of humor. I suggested to him that we would promise each other to invent at least one amusing story daily, about some incident that could happen one day after our liberation. He was a surgeon and had been an assistant on the staff of a large hospital. So I once tried to get him to smile by describing to him how he would be unable to lose the habits of camp life when he returned to his former work. On the building site (especially when the supervisor made his tour of inspection) the foreman encouraged us to work faster by shouting: "Action! Action!" I told my friend, "One day you will be back in the operating room, performing a big abdominal operation. Suddenly an orderly will rush in announcing the arrival of the senior surgeon by shouting, 'Action! Action!' "

Sometimes the other men invented amusing dreams about the future, such as forecasting that during a future dinner engagement they might forget themselves when the soup was served and beg the hostess to ladle it "from the bottom."

The attempt to develop a sense of humor and to see things in a humorous light is some kind of a trick learned while mastering the art of living. Yet it is possible to practice the art of living even in a concentration camp, although suffering is omnipresent. To draw an analogy: a man's suffering is similar to the behavior of gas. If a certain quantity of gas is pumped into an empty chamber, it will fill the chamber completely and evenly, no matter how big the chamber. Thus suffering completely fills the human soul and conscious mind, no matter whether the suffering is great or little. Therefore the "size" of human suffering is absolutely relative.

It also follows that a very trifling thing can cause the greatest of joys. Take as an example something that happened on our journey from Auschwitz to the camp affiliated with Dachau. We had all been afraid that our transport was heading for the Mauthausen camp. We became more and more tense as we approached a certain bridge over the Danube which the train would have to cross to reach Mauthausen, according to the statement of experienced traveling companions. Those who have never seen anything similar cannot possibly imagine the dance of joy performed in the carriage by the prisoners when they saw that our transport was not crossing the bridge and was instead heading "only" for Dachau.

And again, what happened on our arrival in that camp, after a journey lasting two days and three nights? There had not been enough room for everybody to crouch on the floor of the carriage at the same time. The majority of us had to stand all the way, while a few took turns at squatting on the scanty straw which was soaked with human urine. When we arrived the first important news that we heard from older prisoners was that this comparatively small camp (its population was 2,500) had no "oven," no crematorium, no gas! That meant that a person who had become a "Moslem" could not be taken straight to the gas chamber, but would have to wait until a so-called "sick convoy" had been arranged to return to Auschwitz. This joyful surprise put us all in a good mood. The wish of the senior warden of our hut in Auschwitz had come true: we had come, as quickly as possible, to a camp which did not have a "chimney"—unlike Auschwitz. We laughed and cracked jokes in spite of, and during, all we had to go through in the next few hours.

When we new arrivals were counted, one of us was missing. So we had to wait outside in the rain and cold wind until the missing man was found. He was at last discovered in a hut, where he had fallen asleep from exhaustion. Then the roll call was turned into a punishment parade. All through the night and late into the next morning, we had to stand outside, frozen and soaked to the skin after the strain of our long journey. And yet we were all very pleased! There was no chimney in this camp and Auschwitz was a long way off.

Another time we saw a group of convicts pass our work site. How obvious the relativity of all suffering appeared to us then! We envied those prisoners their relatively well-regulated, secure and happy life. They surely had regular opportunities to take baths, we thought sadly. They surely had toothbrushes and clothesbrushes, mattresses—a separate one for each of them—and monthly mail bringing them news of the whereabouts of their relatives, or at least of whether they were still alive or not. We had lost all that a long time ago.

And how we envied those of us who had the opportunity to get into a factory and work in a sheltered room! It was everyone's wish to have such a lifesaving piece of luck. The scale of relative luck extends even further. Even among those detachments outside the camp (in one of which I was a member) there were some units which were considered worse than others. One could envy a man who did not have to wade in deep, muddy clay on a steep slope emptying the tubs of a small field railway for twelve hours daily. Most of the daily accidents occurred on this job, and they were often fatal.

In other work parties the foremen maintained an apparently local tradition of dealing out numerous blows, which made us talk of the relative luck of not being under their command, or perhaps of being under it only temporarily. Once, by an unlucky chance, I got into such a group. If an air raid alarm had not interrupted us after two hours (during which time the foreman had worked on me especially), making it necessary to regroup the workers afterwards, I think that I would have returned to camp on one of the sledges which carried those who had died or were dying from exhaustion. No one can imagine the relief that the siren can bring in such a situation; not even a boxer who has heard the bell signifying the finish of a round and who is thus saved at the last minute from the danger of a knockout.

We were grateful for the smallest of mercies. We were glad when there was time to delouse before going to bed, although in itself this was no pleasure, as it meant standing naked in an unheated hut where icicles hung from the ceiling. But we were thankful if there was no air raid alarm during this operation and the lights were not switched off. If we could not do the job properly, we were kept awake half the night.

The meager pleasures of camp life provided a kind of negative happiness,—"freedom from suffering," as Schopenhauer put it—and even that in a relative way only. Real positive pleasures, even small ones, were very few. I remember drawing up a kind of balance sheet of pleasures one day and finding that in many, many past weeks I had experienced only two pleasurable moments. One occurred when, on returning from work, I was admitted to the cook house after a long wait and was assigned to the line filing up to prisoner-cook F——. He stood behind one of the huge pans and ladled soup into the bowls which were held out to him by the prisoners, who hurriedly filed past. He was the only cook who did not look at the men whose bowls he was filling; the only cook who dealt out the soup equally, regardless of recipient, and who did not make favorites of his personal friends or countrymen, picking out the potatoes for them, while the others got watery soup skimmed from the top.

But it is not for me to pass judgment on those prisoners who put their own people above everyone else. Who can throw a stone at a man who favors his friends under circumstances when, sooner or later, it is a question of life or death? No man should judge unless he asks himself in absolute honesty whether in a similar situation he might not have done the same.

Long after I had resumed normal life again (that means a long time after my release from camp), somebody showed me an illustrated weekly with photographs of prisoners lying crowded on their bunks, staring dully at a visitor. "Isn't this terrible, the dreadful staring faces —everything about it."

"Why?" I asked, for I genuinely did not understand. For at that moment I saw it all again: at 5:00 A.M. it was still pitch dark outside. I was lying on the hard boards in an earthen hut where about seventy of us were "taken care of." We were sick and did not have to leave camp for work; we did not have to go on parade. We could lie all day in our little corner in the hut and doze and wait for the daily distribution of bread (which, of course, was reduced for the sick) and for the daily helping of soup (watered down and also decreased in quantity). But how content we were; happy in spite of everything. While we cowered against each other to avoid any unnecessary loss of warmth, and were too lazy and disinterested to move a finger unnecessarily, we heard shrill whistles and shouts from the square where the night shift had just returned and was assembling for roll call. The door was flung open, and the snowstorm blew into our hut. An exhausted comrade, covered with snow, stumbled inside to sit down for a few minutes. But the senior warden turned him out again. It was strictly forbidden to admit a stranger to a hut while a check-up on the men was in progress. How sorry I was for that fellow and how glad not to be in his skin at that moment, but instead to be sick and able to doze on in the sick quarters! What a life-saver it was to have two days there, and perhaps even two extra days after those!

All this came to my mind when I saw the photographs in the magazine. When I explained, my listeners understood why I did not find the photograph so terrible: the people shown on it might not have been so unhappy after all.

On my fourth day in the sick quarters I had just been detailed to the night shift when the chief doctor rushed in and asked me to volunteer for medical duties in another camp containing typhus patients. Against the urgent advice of my friends (and despite the fact that almost none of my colleagues offered their services), I decided to volunteer. I knew that in a working party I would die in a short time. But if I had to die there might at least be some sense in my death. I thought that it would doubtless be more to the purpose to try and help my comrades as a doctor than to vegetate or finally lose my life as the unproductive laborer that I was then.

For me this was simple mathematics, not sacrifice.

But secretly, the warrant officer from the sanitation squad had ordered that the two doctors who had volunteered for the typhus camp should be "taken care of" till they left. We looked so weak that he feared that he might have two additional corpses on his hands, rather than two doctors.

I mentioned earlier how everything that was not connected with the immediate task of keeping oneself and one's closest friends alive lost its value. Everything was sacrificed to this end. A man's character became involved to the point that he was caught in a mental turmoil which threatened all the values he held and threw them into doubt. Under the influence of a world which no longer recognized the value of human life and human dignity, which had robbed man of his will and had made him an object to be exterminated (having planned, however, to make full use of him first—to the last ounce of his physical resources)—under this influence the personal ego finally suffered a loss of values. If the man in the concentration camp did not struggle against this in a last effort to save his self-respect, he lost the feeling of being an individual, a being with a mind, with inner freedom and personal value. He thought of himself then as only a part of an enormous mass of people; his existence descended to the level of animal life. The men were herded—sometimes to one place then to another; sometimes driven together, then apart—like a flock of sheep without a thought or a will of their own. A small but dangerous pack watched them from all sides, well versed in methods of torture and sadism. They drove the herd incessantly, backwards and forwards, with shouts, kicks and blows. And we, the sheep, thought of two things only—how to evade the bad dogs and how to get a little food.

Just like sheep that crowd timidly into the center of a herd, each of us tried to get into the middle of our formations. That gave one a better chance of avoiding the blows of the guards who were marching on either side and to the front and rear of our column. The central position had the added advantage of affording protection against the bitter winds. It was, therefore, in an attempt to save one's own skin that one literally tried to submerge into the crowd. This was done automatically in the formations. But at other times it was a very conscious effort on our part—in conformity with one of the camp's most imperative laws of self-preservation: Do not be conspicuous. We tried at all times to avoid attracting the attention of the SS.

There were times, of course, when it was possible, and even necessary, to keep away from the crowd. It is well known that an enforced community life, in which attention is paid to everything one does at all times, may result in an irresistible urge to get away, at least for a short while. The prisoner craved to be alone with himself and his thoughts. He yearned for privacy and for solitude. After my transportation to a so-called "rest camp," I had the rare fortune to find solitude for about five minutes at a time. Behind the earthen hut where I worked and in which were crowded about fifty delirious patients, there was a quiet spot in a corner of the double fence of barbed wire surrounding the camp. A tent had been improvised there with a few poles and branches of trees in order to shelter a half-dozen corpses (the daily death rate in the camp).

There was also a shaft leading to the water pipes. I squatted on the wooden lid of this shaft whenever my services were not needed. I just sat and looked out at the green flowering slopes and the distant blue hills of the Bavarian landscape, framed by the meshes of barbed wire. I dreamed longingly, and my thoughts wandered north and northeast, in the direction of my home, but I could only see clouds.

The corpses near me, crawling with lice, did not bother me. Only the steps of passing guards could rouse me from my dreams; or perhaps it would be a call to the sick-bay or to collect a newly arrived supply of medicine for my hut—consisting of perhaps five or ten tablets of aspirin, to last for several days for fifty patients. I collected them and then did my rounds, feeling the patients' pulses and giving half-tablets to the serious cases. But the desperately ill received no medicine. It would not have helped, and besides, it would have deprived those for whom there was still some hope. For light cases, I had nothing, except perhaps a word of encouragement. In this way I dragged myself from patient to patient, though I myself was weak and exhausted from a serious attack of typhus. Then I went back to my lonely place on the wood cover of the water shaft.

This shaft, incidentally, once saved the lives of three fellow prisoners. Shortly before liberation, mass transports were organized to go to Dachau, and these three prisoners wisely tried to avoid the trip. They climbed down the shaft and hid there from the guards. I calmly sat on the lid, looking innocent and playing a childish game of throwing pebbles at the barbed wire. On spotting me, the guard hesitated for a moment, but then passed on. Soon I could tell the three men below that the worst danger was over.

It is very difficult for an outsider to grasp how very little value was placed on human life in camp. The camp inmate was hardened, but possibly became more conscious of this complete disregard of human existence when a convoy of sick men was arranged. The emaciated bodies of the sick were thrown on two-wheeled carts which were drawn by prisoners for many miles, often through snowstorms, to the next camp. If one of the sick men had died before the cart left, he was thrown on anyway—the list had to be correct! The list was the only thing that mattered. A man counted only because he had a prison number. One literally became a number: dead or alive—that was unimportant; the life of a "number" was completely irrelevant. What stood behind that number and that life mattered even less: the fate, the history, the name of the man. In the transport of sick patients that I, in my capacity as a doctor, had to accompany from one camp in Bavaria to another, there was a young prisoner whose brother was not on the list and therefore would have to be left behind. The young man begged so long that the camp warden decided to work an exchange, and the brother took the place of a man who, at the moment, preferred to stay behind. But the list had to be correct! That was easy. The brother just exchanged numbers with the other prisoner.

As I have mentioned before, we had no documents; everyone was lucky to own his body, which, after all, was still breathing. All else about us, i.e., the rags hanging from our gaunt skeletons, was only of interest if we were assigned to a transport of sick patients. The departing "Moslems" were examined with unabashed curiosity to see whether their coats or shoes were not better than one's own. After all, their fates were sealed. But those who stayed behind in camp, who were still capable of some work, had to make use of every means to improve their chances of survival. They were not sentimental. The prisoners saw themselves completely dependent on the moods of the guards—playthings of fate—and this made them even less human than the circumstances warranted.

In Auschwitz I had laid down a rule for myself which proved to be a good one and which most of my comrades later followed. I generally answered all kinds of questions truthfully. But I was silent about anything that was not expressly asked for. If I were asked my age, I gave it. If asked about my profession, I said "doctor," but did not elaborate. The first morning in Auschwitz an SS officer came to the parade ground. We had to fall into separate groups of prisoners over forty years, under forty years, metal workers, mechanics, and so forth. Then we were examined for ruptures and some prisoners had to form a new group. The group that I was in was driven to another hut, where we lined up again. After being sorted out once more and having answered questions as to my age and profession, I was sent to another small group. Once more we were driven to another hut and grouped differently. This continued for some time, and I became quite unhappy, finding myself among strangers who spoke unintelligible foreign languages. Then came the last selection, and I found myself back in the group that had been with me in the first hut! They had barely noticed that I had been sent from hut to hut in the meantime. But I was aware that in those few minutes fate had passed me in many different forms.

When the transport of sick patients for the "rest camp" was organized, my name (that is, my number) was put on the list, since a few doctors were needed. But no one was convinced that the destination was really a rest camp. A few weeks previously the same transport had been prepared. Then, too, everyone had thought that it was destined for the gas ovens. When it was announced that anyone who volunteered for the dreaded night shift would be taken off the transport list, eighty-two prisoners volunteered immediately. A quarter of an hour later the transport was canceled, but the eighty-two stayed on the list for the night shift. For the majority of them, this meant death within the next fortnight.

Now the transport for the rest camp was arranged for the second time. Again no one knew whether this was a ruse to obtain the last bit of work from the sick—if only for fourteen days—or whether it would go to the gas ovens or to a genuine rest camp. The chief doctor, who had taken a liking to me, told me furtively one evening at a quarter to ten, "I have made it known in the orderly room that you can still have your name crossed off the list; you may do so up till ten o'clock."

I told him that this was not my way; that I had learned to let fate take its course. "I might as well stay with my friends," I said. There was a look of pity in his eyes, as if he knew. . . . He shook my hand silently, as though it were a farewell, not for life, but from life. Slowly I walked back to my hut. There I found a good friend waiting for me.

"You really want to go with them?" he asked sadly.

"Yes, I am going."

Tears came to his eyes and I tried to comfort him. Then there was something else to do—to make my will:

"Listen, Otto, if I don't get back home to my wife, and if you should see her again, then tell her that I talked of her daily, hourly. You remember. Secondly, I have loved her more than anyone. Thirdly, the short time I have been married to her outweighs everything, even all we have gone through here."

Otto, where are you now? Are you alive? What has happened to you since our last hour together? Did you find your wife again? And do you remember how I made you learn my will by heart—word for word—in spite of your childlike tears?

The next morning I departed with the transport. This time it was not a ruse. We were not heading for the gas chambers, and we actually did go to a rest camp. Those who had pitied me remained in a camp where famine was to rage even more fiercely than in our new camp. They tried to save themselves, but they only sealed their own fates. Months later, after liberation, I met a friend from the old camp. He related to me how he, as camp policeman, had searched for a piece of human flesh that was missing from a pile of corpses. He confiscated it from a pot in which he found it cooking. Cannibalism had broken out. I had left just in time.

Does this not bring to mind the story of Death in Teheran? A rich and mighty Persian once walked in his garden with one of his servants. The servant cried that he had just encountered Death, who had threatened him. He begged his master to give him his fastest horse so that he could make haste and flee to Teheran, which he could reach that same evening. The master consented and the servant galloped off on the horse. On returning to his house the master himself met Death, and questioned him, "Why did you terrify and threaten my servant?" "I did not threaten him; I only showed surprise in still finding him here when I planned to meet him tonight in Teheran," said Death.

The camp inmate was frightened of making decisions and of taking any sort of initiative whatsoever. This was the result of a strong feeling that fate was one's master, and that one must not try to influence it in any way, but instead let it take its own course. In addition, there was a great apathy, which contributed in no small part to the feelings of the prisoner. At times, lightning decisions had to be made, decisions which spelled life or death. The prisoner would have preferred to let fate make the choice for him. This escape from commitment was most apparent when a prisoner had to make the decision for or against an escape attempt. In those minutes in which he had to make up his mind—and it was always a question of minutes—he suffered the tortures of Hell. Should he make the attempt to flee? Should he take the risk?

I, too, experienced this torment. As the battle-front drew nearer, I had the opportunity to escape. A colleague of mine who had to visit huts outside the camp in the course of his medical duties wanted to escape and take me with him. Under the pretense of holding a consultation about a patient whose illness required a specialist's advice, he smuggled me out. Outside the camp, a member of a foreign resistance movement was to supply us with uniforms and documents. At the last moment there were some technical difficulties and we had to return to camp once more. We used this opportunity to provide ourselves with provisions—a few rotten potatoes—and to look for a rucksack.

We broke into an empty hut of the women's camp, which was vacant, as the women had been sent to another camp. The hut was in great disorder; it was obvious that many women had acquired supplies and fled. There were rags, straw, rotting food, and broken crockery. Some bowls were still in good condition and would have been very valuable to us, but we decided not to take them. We knew that lately, as conditions had become desperate, they had been used not only for food, but also as washbasins and chamber pots. (There was a strictly enforced rule against having any kind of utensil in the hut. However, some people were forced to break this rule, especially the typhus patients, who were much too weak to go outside even with help.) While I acted as a screen, my friend broke into the hut and returned shortly with a rucksack which he hid under his coat. He had seen another one inside which I was to take. So we changed places and I went in. As I searched in the rubbish, finding the rucksack and even a toothbrush, I suddenly saw, among all the things that had been left behind, the body of a woman.

I ran back to my hut to collect all my possessions:

my food bowl, a pair of torn mittens "inherited" from a dead typhus patient, and a few scraps of paper covered with shorthand notes (on which, as I mentioned before, I had started to reconstruct the manuscript which I lost at Auschwitz). I made a quick last round of my patients, who were lying huddled on the rotten planks of wood on either side of the huts. I came to my only countryman, who was almost dying, and whose life it had been my ambition to save in spite of his condition. I had to keep my intention to escape to myself, but my comrade seemed to guess that something was wrong (perhaps I showed a little nervousness). In a tired voice he asked me, "You, too, are getting out?" I denied it, but I found it difficult to avoid his sad look. After my round I returned to him. Again a hopeless look greeted me and somehow I felt it to be an accusation. The unpleasant feeling that had gripped me as soon as I had told my friend I would escape with him became more intense. Suddenly I decided to take fate into my own hands for once. I ran out of the hut and told my friend that I could not go with him. As soon as I had told him with finality that I had made up my mind to stay with my patients, the unhappy feeling left me. I did not know what the following days would bring, but I had gained an inward peace that I had never experienced before. I returned to the hut, sat down on the boards at my countryman's feet and tried to comfort him; then I chatted with the others, trying to quiet them in their delirium.

Our last day in camp arrived. As the battle-front came nearer, mass transports had taken nearly all the prisoners to other camps. The camp authorities, the Capos and the cooks had fled. On this day an order was given that the camp must be evacuated completely by sunset. Even the few remaining prisoners (the sick, a few doctors, and some "nurses") would have to leave. At night, the camp was to be set on fire. In the afternoon the trucks which were to collect the sick had not yet appeared. Instead the camp gates were suddenly closed and the barbed wire closely watched, so that no one could attempt an escape. The remaining prisoners seemed to be destined to burn with the camp. For the second time my friend and I decided to escape.

We had been given an order to bury three men outside the barbed wire fence. We were the only two in camp who had strength enough to do the job. Nearly all the others lay in the few huts which were still in use, prostrate with fever and delirium. We now made our plans: along with the first body we would smuggle out my friend's rucksack, hiding it in the old laundry tub which served as a coffin. When we took out the second body we would also carry out my rucksack, and on the third trip we intended to make our escape. The first two trips went according to plan. After we returned, I waited while my friend tried to find a piece of bread so that we would have something to eat during the next few days in the woods. I waited. Minutes passed. I became more and more impatient as he did not return. After three years of imprisonment, I was picturing freedom joyously, imagining how wonderful it would be like to run toward the battle-front. But we did not get that far.

The very moment when my friend came back, the camp gate was thrown open. A splendid, aluminum-colored car, on which were painted large red crosses, slowly rolled on to the parade ground. A delegate from the Inter-

national Red Cross in Geneva had arrived, and the camp
and its inmates were under his protection. The delegate
billeted himself in a farmhouse in the vicinity, in order to
be near the camp at all times in case of emergency. Who
worried about escape now? Boxes with medicines were
unloaded from the car, cigarettes were distributed, we were
photographed and joy reigned supreme. Now there was
no need for us to risk running toward the fighting line.

In our excitement we had forgotten the third body,
so we carried it outside and dropped it into the narrow
grave we had dug for the three corpses. The guard who
accompanied us—a relatively inoffensive man—suddenly
became quite gentle. He saw that the tables might be
turned and tried to win our goodwill. He joined in the
short prayers that we offered for the dead men before
throwing soil over them. After the tension and excitement
of the past days and hours, those last days in our race with
death, the words of our prayer asking for peace, were as
fervent as any ever uttered by the human voice.

And so the last day in camp passed in anticipation of
freedom. But we had rejoiced too early. The Red Cross
delegate had assured us that an agreement had been signed,
and that the camp must not be evacuated. But that night
the SS arrived with trucks and brought an order to clear
the camp. The last remaining prisoners were to be taken
to a central camp, from which they would be sent to Swit-
zerland within forty-eight hours—to be exchanged for
some prisoners of war. We scarcely recognized the SS.
They were so friendly, trying to persuade us to get in the
trucks without fear, telling us that we should be grateful
for our good luck. Those who were strong enough crowded
into the trucks and the seriously ill and feeble were lifted

up with difficulty. My friend and I—we did not hide our rucksacks now—stood in the last group, from which thirteen would be chosen for the next to last truck. The chief doctor counted out the requisite number, but he omitted the two of us. The thirteen were loaded into the truck and we had to stay behind. Surprised, very annoyed and disappointed, we blamed the chief doctor, who excused himself by saying that he had been tired and distracted. He said that he had thought we still intended to escape. Impatiently we sat down, keeping our rucksacks on our backs, and waited with the few remaining prisoners for the last truck. We had to wait a long time. Finally we lay down on the mattresses of the deserted guard-room, exhausted by the excitement of the last few hours and days, during which we had fluctuated continually between hope and despair. We slept in our clothes and shoes, ready for the journey.

The noise of rifles and cannons woke us; the flashes of tracer bullets and gun shots entered the hut. The chief doctor dashed in and ordered us to take cover on the floor. One prisoner jumped on my stomach from the bed above me with his shoes on. That awakened me all right! Then we grasped what was happening: the battle-front had reached us! The shooting decreased and morning dawned. Outside on the pole at the camp gate a white flag floated in the wind.

Many weeks later we found out that even in those last hours fate had toyed with us few remaining prisoners. We found out just how uncertain human decisions are, especially in matters of life and death. I was confronted with photographs which had been taken in a small camp not far from ours. Our friends who had thought they were traveling to freedom that night had been taken in the trucks to this camp, and there they were locked in the huts and burned to death. Their partially charred bodies were recognizable on the photograph. I thought again of Death in Teheran.

Apart from its role as a defensive mechanism, the prisoners' apathy was also the result of other factors. Hunger and lack of sleep contributed to it (as they do in normal life, also) and to the general irritability which was another characteristic of the prisoners' mental state. The lack of sleep was due partly to the pestering of vermin which infested the terribly overcrowded huts because of the general lack of hygiene and sanitation. The fact that we had neither nicotine nor caffeine also contributed to the state of apathy and irritability.

Besides these physical causes, there were mental ones, in the form of certain complexes. The majority of prisoners suffered from a kind of inferiority complex. We all had once been or had fancied ourselves to be "somebody." Now we were treated like complete nonentities. (The consciousness of one's inner value is anchored in higher, more spiritual things, and cannot be shaken by camp life. But how many free men, let alone prisoners, possess it?) Without consciously thinking about it, the average prisoner felt himself utterly degraded. This became obvious when one observed the contrasts offered by the singular sociological structure of the camp. The more "prominent" prisoners, the Capos, the cooks, the store-keepers and the camp policemen, did not, as a rule, feel degraded at all, like the majority of prisoners, but on the contrary—promoted! Some even developed miniature delusions of grandeur. The mental reaction of the envious and grumbling majority toward this favored minority found expression in several ways, sometimes in jokes. For instance, I heard one prisoner talk to another about a Capo, saying, "Imagine! I knew that man when he was only the president of a large bank. Isn't it fortunate that he has risen so far in the world?"

Whenever the degraded majority and the promoted minority came into conflict (and there were plenty of opportunities for this, starting with the distribution of food) the results were explosive. Therefore, the general irritability (whose physical causes were discussed above) became most intense when these mental tensions were added. It is not surprising that this tension often ended in a general fight. Since the prisoner continually witnessed scenes of beatings, the impulse toward violence was increased. I myself felt my fists clench when anger came over me while I was famished and tired. I was usually very tired, since we had to stoke our stove—which we were allowed to keep in our hut for the typhus patients—throughout the nights. However, some of the most idyllic hours I have ever spent were in the middle of the night when all the others were delirious or sleeping. I could lie stretched out in front of the stove and roast a few pilfered potatoes in a fire made from stolen charcoal. But the following day I always felt even more tired, insensitive and irritable.

While I was working as a doctor in the typhus block, I also had to take the place of the senior block warden who was ill. Therefore, I was responsible to the camp authority for keeping the hut clean—if "clean" can be used to describe such a condition. The pretense at inspection to which the hut was frequently submitted was more for the purpose of torture than of hygiene. More food and a few drugs would have helped, but the only concern of the inspectors was whether a piece of straw was left in the center corridor, or whether the dirty, ragged and verminous blankets of the patients were tucked in neatly at their feet. As to the fate of the inmates, they were quite unconcerned. If I reported smartly, whipping my prison cap from my shorn head and clicking my heels, "Hut number VI/9: 52 patients, two nursing orderlies, and one doctor," they were satisfied. And then they would leave. But until they arrived—often they were hours later than announced, and sometimes did not come at all—I was forced to keep straightening blankets, picking up bits of straw which fell from the bunks, and shouting at the poor devils who tossed in their beds and threatened to upset all my efforts at tidiness and cleanliness. Apathy was particularly increased among the feverish patients, so that they did not react at all unless they were shouted at. Even this failed at times, and then it took tremendous self-control not to strike them. For one's own irritability took on enormous proportions in the face of the other's apathy and especially in the face of the danger (i.e., the approaching inspection) which was caused by it.

In attempting this psychological presentation and a psychopathological explanation of the typical characteristics of a concentration camp inmate, I may give the impression that the human being is completely and un-avoidably influenced by his surroundings. (In this case the surroundings being the unique structure of camp life, which forced the prisoner to conform his conduct to a certain set pattern.) But what about human liberty? Is there no spiritual freedom in regard to behavior and re-action to any given surroundings? Is that theory true which would have us believe that man is no more than a product of many conditional and environmental factors —be they of a biological, psychological or sociological nature? Is man but an accidental product of these? Most important, do the prisoners' reactions to the singular world of the concentration camp prove that man cannot escape the influences of his surroundings? Does man have no choice of action in the face of such circumstances?

We can answer these questions from experience as well as on principle. The experiences of camp life show that man does have a choice of action. There were enough examples, often of a heroic nature, which proved that apathy could be overcome, irritability suppressed. Man *can* preserve a vestige of spiritual freedom, of independence of mind, even in such terrible conditions of psychic and physical stress.

We who lived in concentration camps can remember the men who walked through the huts comforting others, giving away their last piece of bread. They may have been few in number, but they offer sufficient proof that every-thing can be taken from a man but one thing: the last of the human freedoms—to choose one's attitude in any given set of circumstances, to choose one's own way.

And there were always choices to make. Every day, every hour, offered the opportunity to make a decision,

a decision which determined whether you would or would
not submit to those powers which threatened to rob you of
your very self, your inner freedom; which determined
whether or not you would become the plaything of circumstance, renouncing freedom and dignity to become
molded into the form of the typical inmate.

Seen from this point of view, the mental reactions of
the inmates of a concentration camp must seem more to
us than the mere expression of certain physical and sociological conditions. Even though conditions such as lack of
sleep, insufficient food and various mental stresses may
suggest that the inmates were bound to react in certain
ways, in the final analysis it becomes clear that the sort of
person the prisoner became was the result of an inner decision, and not the result of camp influences alone. Funda-
mentally, therefore, any man can, even under such circumstances, decide what shall become of him—mentally
and spiritually. He may retain his human dignity even in
a concentration camp. Dostoevski said once, "There is
only one thing that I dread: not to be worthy of my sufferings." These words frequently came to my mind after I
became acquainted with those martyrs whose behavior
in camp, whose suffering and death, bore witness to the
fact that the last inner freedom cannot be lost. It can be
said that they were worthy of their sufferings; the way
they bore their suffering was a genuine inner achievement.
It is this spiritual freedom—which cannot be taken away
—that makes life meaningful and purposeful.

An active life serves the purpose of giving man the
opportunity to realize values in creative work, while a
passive life of enjoyment affords him the opportunity to
obtain fulfillment in experiencing beauty, art, or nature.

But there is also purpose in that life which is almost barren of both creation and enjoyment and which admits of but one possibility of high moral behavior: namely, in man's attitude to his existence, an existence restricted by external forces. A creative life and a life of enjoyment are banned to him. But not only creativeness and enjoyment are meaningful. If there is a meaning in life at all, then there must be a meaning in suffering. Suffering is an ineradicable part of life, even as fate and death. Without suffering and death human life cannot be complete.

The way in which a man accepts his fate and all the suffering it entails, the way in which he takes up his cross, gives him ample opportunity—even under the most difficult circumstances—to add a deeper meaning to his life. It may remain brave, dignified and unselfish. Or in the bitter fight for self-preservation he may forget his human dignity and become no more than an animal. Here lies the chance for a man either to make use of or to forgo the opportunities of attaining the moral values that a difficult situation may afford him. And this decides whether he is worthy of his sufferings or not.

Do not think that these considerations are unworldly and too far removed from real life. It is true that only a few people are capable of reaching such high moral stand-ards. Of the prisoners only a few kept their full inner liberty and obtained those values which their suffering afforded, but even one such example is sufficient proof that man's inner strength may raise him above his outward fate. Such men are not only in concentration camps. Everywhere man is confronted with fate, with the chance of achieving something through his own suffering.

Take the fate of the sick—especially those who are incurable. I once read a letter written by a young invalid, in which he told a friend that he had just found out he would not live for long, that even an operation would be of no help. He wrote further that he remembered a film he had seen in which a man was portrayed who waited for death in a courageous and dignified way. The boy had thought it a great accomplishment to meet death so well. Now—he wrote—fate was offering him a similar chance.

Those of us who saw the film called *Resurrection*—taken from a book by Tolstoy—years ago, may have had similar thoughts. Here were great destinies and great men. For us, at that time, there was no great fate; there was no chance to achieve such greatness. After the picture we went to the nearest café, and over a cup of coffee and a sandwich we forgot the strange metaphysical thoughts which for one moment had crossed our minds. But when we ourselves were confronted with a great destiny and faced with the decision of meeting it with equal spiritual greatness, by then we had forgotten our youthful resolutions of long ago, and we failed.

Perhaps there came a day for some of us when we saw the same film again, or a similar one. But by then other pictures may have simultaneously unrolled before one's inner eye; pictures of people who attained much more in their lives than a sentimental film could show. Some details of a particular man's inner greatness may have come to one's mind, like the story of the young woman whose death I witnessed in a concentration camp. It is a simple story. There is little to tell and it may sound as if I had invented it; but to me it seems like a poem.

This young woman knew that she would die in the next few days. But when I talked to her she was cheerful in spite of this knowledge. "I am grateful that fate has hit me so hard," she told me. "In my former life I was spoiled and did not take spiritual accomplishments seriously." Pointing through the window of the hut, she said, "This tree here is the only friend I have in my loneliness." Through that window she could see just one branch of a chestnut tree, and on the branch were two blossoms. "I often talk to this tree," she said to me. I was startled and didn't quite know how to take her words. Was she delirious? Did she have occasional hallucinations? Anxiously I asked her if the tree replied. "Yes." What did it say to her? She answered, "It said to me, 'I am here—I am here—I am life, eternal life.'"

We have stated that that which was ultimately responsible for the state of the prisoner's inner self was not so much the enumerated psychophysical causes as it was the result of a free decision. Psychological observations of the prisoners have shown that only the men who allowed their inner hold on their moral and spiritual selves to subside eventually fell victim to the camp's degenerating influences. The question now arises, what could, or should, have constituted this "inner hold"?

Former prisoners, when writing or relating their experiences, agree that the most depressing influence of all was that a prisoner could not know how long his term of imprisonment would be. He had been given no date for his release. (In our camp it was pointless even to talk about it.) Actually a prison term was not only uncertain but unlimited. A well-known research psychologist has pointed out that life in a concentration camp could be called a "provisional existence." We can add to this by defining it as a "provisional existence of unknown limit."

New arrivals usually knew nothing about the conditions at a camp. Those who had come back from other camps were obliged to keep silent, and from some camps no one had returned. On entering camp a change took place in the minds of the men. With the end of uncertainty there came the uncertainty of the end. It was impossible to foresee whether or when, if at all, this form of existence would end.

The latin word *finis* has two meanings: the end or the finish, and a goal to reach. A man who could not see the end of his "provisional existence" was not able to aim at an ultimate goal in life. He ceased living for the future, in contrast to a man in normal life. Therefore the whole structure of his inner life changed; signs of decay set in which we know from other areas of life. The unemployed worker, for example, is in a similar position. His existence has become provisional and in a certain sense he cannot live for the future or aim at a goal. Research work done on unemployed miners has shown that they suffer from a peculiar sort of deformed time—inner time—which is a result of their unemployed state. Prisoners, too, suffered from this strange "time-experience." In camp, a small time unit, a day, for example, filled with hourly tortures and fatigue, appeared endless. A larger time unit, perhaps a week, seemed to pass very quickly. My comrades agreed when I said that in camp a day lasted longer than a week. How paradoxical was our time-experience! In this connection we are reminded of Thomas Mann's *The Magic Mountain*, which contains some very pointed psychological remarks. Mann studies the spiritual

development of people who are in an analogous psychological position, i.e., tuberculosis patients in a sanatorium
who also know no date for their release. They experience a
similar existence—without a future and without a goal.

One of the prisoners, who on his arrival marched with
a long column of new inmates from the station to the camp,
told me later that he had felt as though he were marching
at his own funeral. His life had seemed to him absolutely
without future. He regarded it as over and done, as if he
had already died. This feeling of lifelessness was intensified
by other causes: in time, it was the limitlessness of the
term of imprisonment which was most acutely felt; in
space, the narrow limits of the prison. Anything outside
the barbed wire became remote—out of reach and, in a
way, unreal. The events and the people outside, all the
normal life there, had a ghostly aspect for the prisoner.
The outside life, that is, as much as he could see of it, appeared to him almost as it might have to a dead man who
looked at it from another world.

A man who let himself decline because he could not
see any future goal found himself occupied with retrospective thoughts. In a different connection, we have
already spoken of the tendency there was to look into the
past, to help make the present, with all its horrors, less real.
But in robbing the present of its reality there lay a certain
danger. It became easy to overlook the opportunities to
make something positive of camp life, opportunities which
really did exist. Regarding our "provisional existence" as
unreal was in itself an important factor in causing the
prisoners to lose their hold on life; everything in a way became pointless. Such people forgot that often it is just such
an exceptionally difficult external situation which gives

man the opportunity to grow spiritually beyond himself. Instead of taking the camp's difficulties as a test of
their inner strength, they did not take their life seriously
and despised it as something of no consequence. They preferred to close their eyes and to live in the past. Life for
such people became meaningless.

Naturally only a few people were capable of reaching
great spiritual heights. But a few were given the chance
to attain human greatness even through their apparent
worldly failure and death, an accomplishment which in
ordinary circumstances they would never have achieved.
To the others of us, the mediocre and the half-hearted,
the words of Bismarck could be applied: "Life is like being
at the dentist. You always think that the worst is still to
come, and yet it is over already." Varying this, we could
say that most men in a concentration camp believed that
the real opportunities of life had passed. Yet, in reality,
there was an opportunity and a challenge. One could make
a victory of those experiences, turning life into an inner
triumph, or one could ignore the challenge and simply
vegetate, as did a majority of the prisoners.

Any attempt at fighting the camp's psychopathological influence on the prisoner by psychotherapeutic
or psychohygienic methods had to aim at giving him inner
strength by pointing out to him a future goal to which
he could look forward. Instinctively some of the prisoners
attempted to find one on their own. It is a peculiarity of
man that he can only live by looking to the future— *sub
specie aeternitatis*. And this is his salvation in the most

difficult moments of his existence, although he sometimes has to force his mind to the task.

I remember a personal experience. Almost in tears from pain (I had terrible sores on my feet from wearing torn shoes), I limped a few kilometers with our long column of men from the camp to our work site. Very cold, bitter winds struck us. I kept thinking of the endless little problems of our miserable life. What would there be to eat tonight? If a piece of sausage came as extra ration, should I exchange it for a piece of bread? Should I trade my last cigarette, which was left from a bonus I received a fortnight ago, for a bowl of soup? How could I get a piece of wire to replace the fragment which served as one of my shoelaces? Would I get to our work site in time to join my usual working party or would I have to join another, which might have a brutal foreman? What could I do to get on good terms with the Capo, who could help me to obtain work in camp instead of undertaking this horribly long daily march?

I became disgusted with the state of affairs which compelled me, daily and hourly, to think of only such trivial things. I forced my thoughts to turn to another subject. Suddenly I saw myself standing on the platform of a well-lit, warm and pleasant lecture room. In front of me sat an attentive audience on comfortable upholstered seats. I was giving a lecture on the psychology of the concentration camp! All that oppressed me at that moment became objective, seen and described from the remote viewpoint of science. By this method I succeeded somehow in rising above the situation, above the sufferings of the moment, and I observed them as if they were already of the past. Both I and my troubles became the object of an interesting psychoscientific study undertaken by myself. What does Spinoza say in his *Ethics?*—*"Affectus, qui passio est, desinit esse passio simulatque eius claram et distinctam formamus ideam."* Emotion, which is suffering, ceases to be suffering as soon as we form a clear and precise picture of it.

The prisoner who had lost faith in the future—his future—was doomed. With his loss of belief in the future, he also lost his spiritual hold; he let himself decline and became subject to mental and physical decay. Usually this happened quite suddenly, in the form of a crisis, the symptoms of which were familiar to the experienced camp inmate. We all feared this moment—not for ourselves, which would have been pointless, but for our friends. Usually it began with the prisoner refusing one morning to get dressed and wash or to go out on the parade grounds. No entreaties, no blows, no threats had any effect. He just lay there, hardly moving. If this crisis was brought about by an illness, he refused to be taken to the sick-bay or to do anything to help himself. He simply gave up. There he remained, lying in his own excreta, and nothing bothered him any more.

I once had a dramatic demonstration of the close link between the loss of faith in the future and this dangerous giving up. F——, my senior block warden, a fairly well-known composer and librettist, confided in me one day: "I would like to tell you something, Doctor. I have had a strange dream. A voice told me that I could wish for something, that I should only say what I wanted to know, and all my questions would be answered. What do you think I asked? That I would like to know when the war would be over for me. You know what I mean, Doctor—for me! I wanted to know when we, when our camp, would be liberated and our sufferings come to an end."

"And when did you have this dream?" I asked.

"In February, 1945," he answered. It was then the beginning of March.

"What did your dream voice answer?"

Furtively he whispered to me, "March thirtieth."

When F—— told me about his dream, he was still full of hope and convinced that the voice of his dream would be right. But as the promised day drew nearer, the war news which reached our camp made it appear very unlikely that we would be free on the promised date. On March twenty-ninth, F—— suddenly became ill and ran a high temperature. On March thirtieth, the day his prophecy had told him that the war and suffering would be over for him, he became delirious and lost consciousness. On March thirty-first, he was dead. To all outward appearances, he had died of typhus.

Those who know how close the connection is between the state of mind of a man—his courage and hope, or lack of them—and the state of immunity of his body will understand that the sudden loss of hope and courage can have a deadly effect. The ultimate cause of my friend's death was that the expected liberation did not come and he was severely disappointed. This suddenly lowered his body's resistance against the latent typhus infection. His faith in the future and his will to live had become paralyzed and his body fell victim to illness—and thus the voice of his dream was right after all.

The observations of this one case and the conclusion drawn from them are in accordance with something that was drawn to my attention by the chief doctor of our concentration camp. The death rate in the week between Christmas, 1944, and New Year's, 1945, increased in camp beyond all previous experience. In his opinion, the explanation for this increase did not lie in the harder working conditions or the deterioration of our food supplies or a change of weather or new epidemics. It was simply that the majority of the prisoners had lived in the naïve hope that they would be home again by Christmas. As the time drew near and there was no encouraging news, the prisoners lost courage and disappointment overcame them. This had a dangerous influence on their powers of resistance and a great number of them died.

As we said before, any attempt to restore a man's inner strength in the camp had first to succeed in showing him some future goal. Nietzsche's words, "He who has a why to live for can bear with almost any how," could be the guiding motto for all psychotherapeutic and psycho-hygienic efforts regarding prisoners. Whenever there was an opportunity for it, one had to give them a why—an aim—for their lives, in order to strengthen them to bear the terrible how of their existence. Woe to him who saw no more sense in his life, no aim, no purpose, and therefore no point in carrying on. He was soon lost. The typical reply with which such a man rejected all encouraging arguments was, "I have nothing to expect from life any more." What sort of answer can one give to that?

What was really needed was a fundamental change in our attitude toward life. We had to learn ourselves and, furthermore, we had to teach the despairing men, that *it did not really matter what we expected from life, but rather what life expected from us.* We needed to stop asking about the meaning of life, and instead to think of ourselves as those who were being questioned by life—daily and hourly. Our answer must consist, not in talk and meditation, but in right action and in right conduct. Life ultimately means taking the responsibility to find the right answer to its problems and to fulfill the tasks which it constantly sets for each individual.

These tasks, and therefore the meaning of life, differ from man to man, and from moment to moment. Thus it is impossible to define the meaning of life in a general way. Questions about the meaning of life can never be answered by sweeping statements. "Life" does not mean something vague, but something very real and concrete, just as life's tasks are also very real and concrete. They form man's destiny, which is different and unique for each individual. No man and no destiny can be compared with any other man or any other destiny. No situation repeats itself, and each situation calls for a different response. Sometimes the situation in which a man finds himself may require him to shape his own fate by action. At other times it is more advantageous for him to make use of an opportunity for contemplation and to realize assets in this way. Sometimes man may be required simply to accept fate, to bear his cross. Every situation is distinguished by its uniqueness, and there is always only one right answer to the problem posed by the situation at hand.

When a man finds that it is his destiny to suffer, he will have to accept his suffering as his task; his single and unique task. He will have to acknowledge the fact that even in suffering he is unique and alone in the universe. No one can relieve him of his suffering or suffer in his place. His unique opportunity lies in the way in which he bears his burden.

For us, as prisoners, these thoughts were not speculations far removed from reality. They were the only thoughts that could be of help to us. They kept us from despair, even when there seemed to be no chance of coming out of it alive. Long ago we had passed the stage of asking what was the meaning of life, a naïve query which understands life as the attaining of some aim through the active creation of something of value. For us, the meaning of life embraced the wider cycles of life and death, of suffering and of dying.

Once the meaning of suffering had been revealed to us, we refused to minimize or alleviate the camp's tortures by ignoring them or harboring false illusions and entertaining artificial optimism. Suffering had become a task on which we did not want to turn our backs. We had realized its hidden opportunities for achievement, the opportunities which caused the poet Rilke to write, *"Wie viel ist aufzuleiden!"* (How much suffering there is to get through!) Rilke spoke of "getting through suffering" as others would talk of "getting through work." There was plenty of suffering for us to get through. Therefore, it was necessary to face up to the full amount of suffering, trying to keep moments of weakness and furtive tears to a minimum. But there was no need to be ashamed of tears, for tears bore witness that a man had the greatest of courage, the courage to suffer. Only very few realized that. Shamefacedly some confessed occasionally that they had wept, like the comrade who answered my question of how he had gotten over his edema, by confessing, "I have wept it out of my system."

The tender beginnings of a psychotherapy or psycho-hygiene were, when they were possible at all in the camp, either individual or collective in nature. The individual psychotherapeutic attempts were often a kind of "life-saving procedure." These efforts were usually concerned with the prevention of suicides. A very strict camp ruling forbade any efforts to save a man who attempted suicide. It was forbidden, for example, to cut down a man who was trying to hang himself. Therefore, it was all important to prevent these attempts from occurring.

I remember two cases of would-be suicide, which bore a striking similarity to each other. Both men had talked of their intentions to commit suicide. Both used the typical argument—they had nothing more to expect from life. In both cases it was a question of getting them to realize that life was still expecting something from them; something in the future was expected of them. We found, in fact, that for the one it was his child whom he adored and who was waiting for him in a foreign country. For the other it was a thing, not a person. This man was a scientist and had written a series of books which still needed to be finished. His work could not be done by any-one else, any more than another person could ever take the place of the father in his child's affections.

This uniqueness and singleness which distinguishes

each individual and gives a meaning to his existence has a bearing on creative work as much as it does on human love. When the impossibility of replacing a person is realized, it allows the responsibility which a man has for his existence and its continuance to appear in all its magnitude. A man who becomes conscious of the responsibility he bears toward a human being who affectionately waits for him, or to an unfinished work, will never be able to throw away his life. He knows the "why" for his existence, and will be able to bear almost any "how."

The opportunities for collective psychotherapy were naturally limited in camp. The right example was more effective than words could ever be. A senior block warden who did not side with the authorities had, by his just and encouraging behavior, a thousand opportunities to exert a far-reaching moral influence on those under his jurisdiction. The immediate influence of behavior is always more effective than that of words. But at times a word was effective too, when mental receptiveness had been intensified by some outer circumstances. I remember an incident when there was occasion for psychotherapeutic work on the inmates of a whole hut, due to an intensification of their receptiveness because of a certain external situation.

It had been a bad day. On parade, an announcement had been made about the many actions that would, from then on, be regarded as sabotage and therefore punishable by immediate death by hanging. Among these were crimes such as cutting small strips from our old blankets (in order to improvise ankle supports) and very minor "thefts." A few days previously a semi-starved prisoner had broken into the potato store to steal a few pounds of potatoes. The theft had been discovered and some prisoners had recognized the "burglar." When the camp authorities heard about it they ordered that the guilty man be given up to them or the whole camp would starve for a day. Naturally the 2,500 men preferred to fast.

On the evening of this day of fasting we lay in our earthen huts—in a very low mood. Very little was said and every word sounded irritable. Then, to make matters even worse, the light went out. Tempers reached their lowest ebb. But our senior block warden was a wise man. He improvised a little talk about all that was on our minds at that moment. He talked about the many comrades who had died in the last few days, either of sickness or of suicide. But he also mentioned what may have been the real reason for their deaths: giving up hope. He maintained that there should be some way of preventing possible future victims from reaching this extreme state. And it was to me that the warden pointed to give this advice.

God knows, I was not in the mood to give psychological explanations or to preach any sermons—to offer my comrades a kind of medical care of their souls. I was cold and hungry, irritable and tired, but I had to make the effort and use this unique opportunity. Encouragement was now more necessary than ever.

So I began by mentioning the most trivial of comforts first. I said that even in this Europe in the sixth winter of the Second World War, our situation was not the most terrible we could think of. I said that each of us had to ask himself what irreplaceable losses he had suffered up

to then. I speculated that for most of them these losses
had really been few. Whoever was still alive had reason
for hope. Health, family, happiness, professional abili-
ties, fortune, position in society—all these were things that
could be achieved again or restored. After all, we still had
all our bones intact. Whatever we had gone through could
still be an asset to us in the future. And I quoted from
Nietzsche: "*Was mich nicht umbringt, macht mich
stärker.*" (That which does not kill me, makes me
stronger.)

Then I spoke about the future. I said that to the im-
partial the future must seem hopeless. I agreed that
each of us could guess for himself how small were
his chances of survival. I told them that although there
was still no typhus epidemic in the camp, I estimated my
own chances at about one in twenty. But I also told them
that, in spite of this, I had no intention of losing hope
and giving up. For no man knew what the future would
bring, much less the next hour. Even if we could not expect any sensational military events in the next few days,
who knew better than we, with our experience of camps,
how great chances sometimes opened up, quite suddenly, at least for the individual. For instance, one might
be attached unexpectedly to a special group with exceptionally good working conditions—for this was the kind of
thing which constituted the "luck" of the prisoner.

But I did not only talk of the future and the veil
which was drawn over it. I also mentioned the past; all
its joys, and how its light shone even in the present darkness. Again I quoted a poet—to avoid sounding like a
preacher myself—who had written, "*Was Du erlebst,
kann keine Macht der Welt Dir rauben.*" (What you

have experienced, no power on earth can take from you.)
Not only our experiences, but all we have done, whatever
great thoughts we may have had, and all we have suffered,
all this is not lost, though it is past; we have brought it into being. Having been is also a kind of being, and perhaps
the surest kind.

Then I spoke of the many opportunities of giving life
a meaning. I told my comrades (who lay motionless, although occasionally a sigh could be heard) that human
life, under any circumstances, never ceases to have a meaning, and that this infinite meaning of life includes
suffering and dying, privation and death. I asked the
poor creatures who listened to me attentively in the
darkness of the hut to face up to the seriousness of our
position. They must not lose hope but should keep their
courage in the certainty that the hopelessness of our struggle did not detract from its dignity and its meaning. I
said that someone looks down on each of us in difficult
hours—a friend, a wife, somebody alive or dead, or a
God—and he would not expect us to disappoint him. He
would hope to find us suffering proudly—not miserably
—knowing how to die.

And finally I spoke of our sacrifice, which had meaning in every case. It was in the nature of this sacrifice
that it should appear to be pointless in the normal world,
the world of material success. But in reality our sacrifice
did have a meaning. Those of us who had any religious
faith, I said frankly, could understand without difficulty.
I told them of a comrade who on his arrival in camp had
tried to make a pact with Heaven that his suffering and
death should save the human being he loved from a painful end. For this man, suffering and death were meaning-

ful; his was a sacrifice of the deepest significance. <u>He did
not want to die for nothing.</u> None of us wanted that.

The purpose of my words was to find a full meaning
in our life, then and there, in that hut and in that practically hopeless situation. I saw that my efforts had been
successful. When the electric bulb flared up again, I saw
the miserable figures of my friends limping toward me to
thank me with tears in their eyes. But I have to confess
here that only too rarely had I the inner strength to make
contact with my companions in suffering and that I must
have missed many opportunities for doing so.

We now come to the third stage of a prisoner's mental reactions: the psychology of the prisoner after his liberation. But prior to that we shall consider a question
which the psychologist is asked frequently, especially
when he has personal knowledge of these matters: What
can you tell us about the psychological make-up of the
camp guards? How is it possible that men of flesh and
blood could treat others as so many prisoners say they have
been treated? Having once heard these accounts and having come to believe that these things did happen, one
is bound to ask how, psychologically, they could happen.
To answer this question without going into great detail, a
few things must be pointed out:

First, among the guards there were some sadists, sadists
in the purest clinical sense.

Second, these sadists were always selected when a really
severe detachment of guards was needed.

There was great joy at our work site when we had

permission to warm ourselves for a few minutes (after two hours of work in the bitter frost) in front of a little stove which was fed with twigs and scraps of wood. But there were always some foremen who found a great pleasure in taking this comfort from us. How clearly their faces reflected this pleasure when they not only forbade us to stand there but turned over the stove and dumped its lovely fire into the snow! When the SS took a dislike to a person, there was always some special man in their ranks known to have a passion for, and to be highly specialized in, sadistic torture, to whom the unfortunate prisoner was sent.

Third, the feelings of the majority of the guards had been dulled by the number of years in which, in ever-increasing doses, they had witnessed the brutal methods of the camp. These morally and mentally hardened men at least refused to take active part in sadistic measures. But they did not prevent others from carrying them out.

Fourth, it must be stated that even among the guards there were some who took pity on us. I shall only mention the commander of the camp from which I was liberated. It was found after the liberation—only the camp doctor, a prisoner himself, had known of it previously—that this man had paid no small sum of money from his own pocket in order to purchase medicines for his prisoners from the nearest market town.[1] But the senior camp warden, a

[1] An interesting incident with reference to this SS commander is in regard to the attitude toward him of some of his Jewish prisoners. At the end of the war when the American troops liberated the prisoners from our camp, three young Hungarian Jews hid this commander in the Bavarian woods. Then they went to the commandant of the American Forces who was very eager to capture this SS commander and they said they would tell him where he was but only under certain conditions: the American commander must

prisoner himself, was harder than any of the SS guards. He beat the other prisoners at every slightest opportunity, while the camp commander, to my knowledge, never once lifted his hand against any of us.

It is apparent that the mere knowledge that a man was either a camp guard or a prisoner tells us almost nothing. Human kindness can be found in all groups, even those which as a whole it would be easy to condemn. The boundaries between groups overlapped and we must not try to simplify matters by saying that these men were angels and those were devils. Certainly, it was a considerable achievement for a guard or foreman to be kind to the prisoners in spite of all the camp's influences, and, on the other hand, the baseness of a prisoner who treated his own companions badly was exceptionally contemptible. Obviously the prisoners found the lack of character in such men especially upsetting, while they were profoundly moved by the smallest kindness received from any of the guards. I remember how one day a foreman secretly gave me a piece of bread which I knew he must have saved from his breakfast ration. It was far more than the small piece of bread which moved me to tears at that time. It was the human "something" which this man also gave to me—the word and look which accompanied the gift.

From all this we may learn that there are two races

---

promise that absolutely no harm would come to this man. After a while, the American officer finally promised these young Jews that the SS commander when taken into captivity would be kept safe from harm. Not only did the American officer keep his promise but, as a matter of fact, the former SS commander of this concentration camp was in a sense restored to his command, for he supervised the collection of clothing among the nearby Bavarian villages, and its distribution to all of us who at that time still wore the clothes we had inherited from other inmates of Camp Auschwitz who were not as fortunate as we, having been sent to the gas chamber immediately upon their arrival at the railway station.

of men in this world, but only these two—the "race" of the decent man and the "race" of the indecent man. Both are found everywhere; they penetrate into all groups of society. No group consists entirely of decent or indecent people. In this sense, no group is of "pure race"—and therefore one occasionally found a decent fellow among the camp guards.

Life in a concentration camp tore open the human soul and exposed its depths. Is it surprising that in those depths we again found only human qualities which in their very nature were a mixture of good and evil? The rift dividing good from evil, which goes through all human beings, reaches into the lowest depths and becomes apparent even on the bottom of the abyss which is laid open by the concentration camp.

And now to the last chapter in the psychology of a concentration camp—the psychology of the prisoner who has been released. In describing the experiences of liberation, which naturally must be personal, we shall pick up the threads of that part of our narrative which told of the morning when the white flag was hoisted above the camp gates, after days of high tension. This state of inner suspense was followed by total relaxation. But it would be quite wrong to think that we went mad with joy. What, then, did happen?

With tired steps we prisoners dragged ourselves to the camp gates. Timidly we looked around and glanced at each other questioningly. Then we ventured a few steps out of camp. This time no orders were shouted at us, nor was there any need to duck quickly to avoid a blow or kick. Oh no! This time the guards offered us cigarettes! We hardly recognized them at first; they had hurriedly changed into civilian clothes. We walked slowly along the road leading from the camp. Soon our legs hurt and threatened to buckle. But we limped on; we wanted to see the camp's surroundings for the first time with the eyes of free men. "Freedom"—we repeated to ourselves, and yet we could not grasp it. We had said this word so often during all the years we dreamed about it, that it had lost its meaning. Its reality did not penetrate into our consciousness; we could not grasp the fact that freedom was ours.

We came to meadows full of flowers. We saw and realized that they were there, but we had no feelings about them. The first spark of joy came when we saw a rooster with a tail of multicolored feathers. But it remained only a spark; we did not yet belong to this world.

In the evening when we all met again in our hut, one said secretly to the other, "Tell me, were you pleased today?"

And the other replied, feeling ashamed as he did not know that we all felt similarly, "Truthfully, no!" We had literally lost the ability to feel pleased and had to relearn it slowly.

Psychologically, what was happening to the liberated prisoners could be called "depersonalization." Everything appeared unreal, unlikely, as in a dream. We could not believe it was true. How often in the past years had we been deceived by dreams! We dreamt that the day of liberation had come, that we had been set free, had returned home, greeted our friends, embraced our wives, sat down at the table and started to tell of all the things we had gone through—even of how we had often seen the day of liberation in our dreams. And then—a whistle shrilled in our ears, the signal to get up, and our dreams of freedom came to an end. And now the dream had come true. But could we truly believe in it?

The body has fewer inhibitions than the mind. It made good use of the new freedom from the first moment on. It began to eat ravenously, for hours and days, even half the night. It is amazing what quantities one can eat. And when one of the prisoners was invited out by a friendly farmer in the neighborhood, he ate and ate and then drank coffee, which loosened his tongue, and he then began to talk, often for hours. The pressure which had been on his mind for years was released at last. Hearing him talk, one got the impression that he *had* to talk, that his desire to speak was irresistible. I have known people who have been under heavy pressure only for a short time (for example, through a cross-examination by the Gestapo) to have similar reactions. Many days passed, until not only the tongue was loosened, but something within oneself as well; then feeling suddenly broke through the strange fetters which had restrained it.

One day, a few days after the liberation, I walked through the country past flowering meadows, for miles and miles, toward the market town near the camp. Larks rose to the sky and I could hear their joyous song. There

was no one to be seen for miles around; there was nothing
but the wide earth and sky and the larks' jubilation and
the freedom of space. I stopped, looked around, and up to
the sky—and then I went down on my knees. At that
moment there was very little I knew of myself or of the
world—I had but one sentence in mind—always the same:
"I called to the Lord from my narrow prison and He
answered me in the freedom of space."

How long I knelt there and repeated this sentence
memory can no longer recall. But I know that on that
day, in that hour, my new life started. Step for step I pro-
gressed, until I again became a human being.

The way that led from the acute mental tension of
the last days in camp (from that war of nerves to mental
peace) was certainly not free from obstacles. It would be
an error to think that a liberated prisoner was not in need
of spiritual care any more. We have to consider that a man
who has been under such enormous mental pressure for
such a long time is naturally in some danger after his liberation, especially since the pressure was released quite suddenly. This danger (in the sense of psychological hygiene)
is the psychological counterpart of the bends. Just as the
physical health of the caisson worker would be endangered
if he left his diver's chamber suddenly (where he is under
enormous atmospheric pressure), so the man who has suddenly been liberated from mental pressure can suffer damage to his moral and spiritual health.

During this psychological phase one observed that
people with natures of a more primitive kind could not

escape the influences of the brutality which had surrounded them in camp life. Now, being free, they thought they could use their freedom licentiously and ruthlessly. The only thing that had changed for them was that they were now the oppressors instead of the oppressed. They became instigators, not objects, of willful force and injustice. They justified their behavior by their own terrible experiences. This was often revealed in apparently insignificant events. A friend was walking across a field with me toward the camp when suddenly we came to a field of green crops. Automatically, I avoided it, but he drew his arm through mine and dragged me through it. I stammered something about not treading down the young crops. He became annoyed, gave me an angry look and shouted, "You don't say! And hasn't enough been taken from us? My wife and child have been gassed—not to mention everything else—and you would forbid me to tread on a few stalks of oats!"

Only slowly could these men be guided back to the commonplace truth that no one has the right to do wrong, not even if wrong has been done to them. We had to strive to lead them back to this truth, or the consequences would have been much worse than the loss of a few thousand stalks of oats. I can still see the prisoner who rolled up his shirt sleeves, thrust his right hand under my nose and shouted, "May this hand be cut off if I don't stain it with blood on the day when I get home!" I want to emphasize that the man who said these words was not a bad fellow. He had been the best of comrades in camp and afterwards.

Apart from the moral deformity resulting from the sudden release of mental pressure, there were two other fundamental experiences which threatened to damage the character of the liberated prisoner: bitterness and disillusionment when he returned to his former life.

Bitterness was caused by a number of things he came up against in his former home town. When, on his return, a man found that in many places he was met only with a shrug of the shoulders and with hackneyed phrases, he tended to become bitter and to ask himself why he had gone through all that he had. When he heard the same phrases nearly everywhere—"We did not know about it," and "We, too, have suffered," then he asked himself, have they really nothing better to say to me?

The experience of disillusionment is different. Here it was not one's fellow man (whose superficiality and lack of feeling was so disgusting that one finally felt like creeping into a hole and neither hearing nor seeing human beings any more) but fate itself which seemed so cruel. A man who for years had thought he had reached the absolute limit of all possible suffering now found that suffering has no limits, and that he could suffer still more, and still more intensely.

When we spoke about attempts to give a man in camp mental courage, we said that he had to be shown something to look forward to in the future. He had to be reminded that life still waited for him, that a human being waited for his return. But after liberation? There were some men who found that no one awaited them. Woe to him who found that the person whose memory alone had given him courage in camp did not exist any more! Woe to him who, when the day of his dreams finally came, found it so different from all he had longed for! Perhaps he boarded a trolley, traveled out to the home which he had seen for years in his mind, and only in his mind, and pressed the bell, just as he has longed to do in thousands of dreams, only to find that the person who should open the door was not there, and would never be there again.

We all said to each other in camp that there could be no earthly happiness which could compensate for all we had suffered. We were not hoping for happiness—it was not that which gave us courage and gave meaning to our suffering, our sacrifices and our dying. And yet we were not prepared for unhappiness. This disillusionment, which awaited not a small number of prisoners, was an experience which these men have found very hard to get over and which, for a psychiatrist, is also very difficult to help them overcome. But this must not be a discouragement to him; on the contrary, it should provide an added stimulus.

But for every one of the liberated prisoners, the day comes when, looking back on his camp experiences, he can no longer understand how he endured it all. As the day of his liberation eventually came, when everything seemed to him like a beautiful dream, so also the day comes when all his camp experiences seem to him nothing but a nightmare.

The crowning experience of all, for the homecoming man, is the wonderful feeling that, after all he has suffered, there is nothing he need fear any more—except his God.

Part Two

Basic Concepts of Logotherapy

Readers of my short autobiographical story usually ask for a fuller and more direct explanation of my therapeutic doctrine. Accordingly I added a brief section on logotherapy to the original edition of *From Death-Camp to Existentialism.* But that was not enough, and I have been besieged by requests for a more extended treatment. Therefore in the present edition I have completely rewritten and considerably expanded my account.

The assignment was not easy. To convey to the reader within a short space all the material which required seventeen volumes in German is an almost hopeless task. I am reminded of the American doctor who once turned up in my clinic in Vienna and asked me, "Now, doctor, are you a psychoanalyst?" Whereupon I replied, "Not exactly a psychoanalyst; let's say a psychotherapist." Then he continued questioning me: "What school do you stand for?" I answered, "It is my own theory; it is called *logotherapy.*" "Can you tell me in one sentence what is meant by logotherapy?" he asked. "At least, what is the difference between psychoanalysis and logotherapy?" "Yes," I said, "but in the first place, can you tell me in one sentence what you think the essence of psychoanalysis is?" This was his answer: "During psychoanalysis, the patient must lie down on a couch and tell you things which sometimes are very disagreeable to tell." Whereupon I immediately retorted with the following improvisation: "Now, in logotherapy the patient may remain sitting erect but he must hear things which sometimes are very disagreeable to hear."

Of course, this was meant facetiously and not as a capsule version of logotherapy. However, there is something in it, inasmuch as logotherapy, in comparison with psychoanalysis, is a method less *retrospective* and less *introspective*. Logotherapy focuses rather on the future, that is to say, on the assignments and meanings to be fulfilled by the patient in his future. At the same time, logotherapy de-focuses all the vicious circle formations and feedback mechanisms which play such a great role in the development of neuroses. Thus, the typical self-centeredness of the neurotic is broken up instead of being continually fostered and reinforced.

To be sure, this kind of statement is an oversimplification; yet, in logotherapy the patient is actually confronted with and reoriented toward the meaning of his life. My improvisation of a definition of what logotherapy means, therefore, holds true in that the truly neurotic individual does try to escape the full awareness of his life task. And to make him aware of this task, to awaken him to a fuller consciousness of it, can contribute much to his ability to overcome his neurosis.

Let me explain why I have employed the term "logotherapy" as the name for my theory. *Logos* is a Greek word which denotes "meaning." Logotherapy or, as it has been called by some authors, "The Third Viennese School of Psychotherapy," focuses on the meaning of human existence as well as on man's search for such a meaning. According to logotherapy, this striving to find a meaning in one's life is the primary motivational force in man. That is why I speak of a *will to meaning* in contrast to the pleasure principle (or, as we could also term it, the *will to pleasure*) on which Freudian psychoanalysis is centered, as well in contrast to the *will to power* stressed by Adlerian psychology.

The Will to Meaning

Man's search for meaning is a primary force in his life and not a "secondary rationalization" of instinctual drives. This meaning is unique and specific in that it must and can be fulfilled by him alone; only then does it achieve a significance which will satisfy his own *will* to meaning. There are some authors who contend that meanings and values are "nothing but defense mechanisms, reaction formations and sublimations." But as for myself, I would not be willing to live merely for the sake of my "defense mechanisms," nor would I be ready to die merely for the sake of my "reaction formations." Man, however, is able to live and even to die for the sake of his ideals and values!

A statistical survey of 7,948 students at 48 colleges was conducted by social scientists from Johns Hopkins University. Their preliminary report is part of a two-year study sponsored by the National Institute of Mental

Health. Asked what they considered "very important" to them now, 16 per cent of the students checked "making a lot of money"; 78 per cent said their first goal was "finding a purpose and meaning to my life."

Of course, there may be some cases in which an individual's concern with values is really a camouflage of hidden inner conflicts; but, if so, they represent the exceptions from the rule rather than the rule itself. In these instances a psychodynamic interpretation is justified in an attempt to disclose the underlying unconscious dynamics. In such cases we have actually to deal with pseudo-values (a good example of this is that of the bigot), and as such they have to be unmasked. Unmasking, or debunking, however, should stop as soon as one is confronted with what is authentic and genuine in man, e.g., man's desire for a life that is as meaningful as possible. If it does not stop then, the man who does the debunking merely betrays his own will to depreciate the spiritual aspirations of another.

We have to beware of the tendency to deal with values in terms of mere self-expression of man himself. For *logos*, or "meaning," is not only an emerging from existence itself but rather something confronting existence. If the meaning which is waiting to be fulfilled by man were really nothing but a mere expression of self, or no more than a projection of his wishful thinking, it would immediately lose its demanding and challenging characters; it could no longer call man forth or summon him. This holds true not only for the so-called sublimation of instinctual drives but for what C. G. Jung called the "archetypes" of the "collective unconscious" as well, inasmuch as the latter would also be self-expressions, namely, of mankind as a whole. This holds true as well for the contention of some existentialist thinkers who see in man's ideals nothing but his own inventions. According to Jean-Paul Sartre, man invents himself, he designs his own "essence"; that is to say, what he essentially is, including what he should be, or ought to become. However, I think the meaning of our existence is not invented by ourselves, but rather detected.

Psychodynamic research in the field of values is legitimate; the question is whether it is always appropriate. Above all, we must keep in mind that any exclusively psychodynamic investigation can, in principle, only reveal what is a driving force in man. Values, however, do not drive a man; they do not *push* him, but rather *pull* him. This is a difference, by the way, of which I am constantly reminded whenever I go through the doors of an American hotel. One of them has to be pulled while the other has to be pushed. Now, if I say man is *pulled* by values, what is implicitly referred to is the fact that there is always freedom involved: the freedom of man to make his choice between accepting or rejecting an offer, i.e., to fulfill a meaning potentiality, or else to forfeit it.

However, it should be made quite clear that there cannot exist in man any such thing as a *moral drive,* or even a *religious drive,* in the same manner as we speak of man's being determined by basic instincts. Man is never driven to moral behavior; in each instance, he decides to behave morally. Man does not do so in order to satisfy a moral drive and to have a good conscience. Man does not behave morally for the sake of having a good conscience but for the sake of a cause to which he commits himself, or for a person whom he loves, or for the sake of his God. If he actually did it for the sake of having a good conscience, he would become a case of Pharisaism and cease to be a truly moral person. I think that even the saints did not care for anything other than simply to serve God, and I doubt that they ever had it in mind to become saints. If that were the case they would have become only perfectionists rather than saints. Certainly, "a good conscience is the best pillow," as a German saying goes; but true morality is more than just a sleeping pill, or a tranquilizing drug.

Existential Frustration

Man's will to meaning can also be frustrated, in which case logotherapy speaks of "existential frustration." The term "existential" may be used in three ways: to refer to (1) *existence* itself, i.e., the specifically human mode of being; (2) the *meaning* of existence; and (3) the striving to find a concrete meaning in personal existence, that is to say, the *will* to meaning.

Existential frustration can also result in neuroses. For this type of neuroses, logotherapy has coined the term "noögenic neuroses" in contrast to neuroses in the usual sense of the word, i.e., psychogenic neuroses. Noögenic neuroses have their origin not in the psychological but rather in the "noölogical" (from the Greek "noos" meaning mind) dimension of the human existence. This is another logotherapeutic term which denotes anything pertaining to the "spiritual" core of man's personality. It must be kept in mind, however, that within the frame of reference of logotherapy, "spiritual" does not have a primarily religious connotation but refers to the specifically human dimension.

Noögenic Neuroses

Noögenic neuroses do not emerge from conflicts between drives and instincts but rather from conflicts between various values; in other words, from moral conflicts, or, to speak in a more general way, from spiritual problems. Among such problems, existential frustration often plays a large role.

It is obvious that in noögenic cases the appropriate and adequate therapy is not psychotherapy in general but rather logotherapy; a therapy, that is, which dares to enter the spiritual dimension of human existence. In fact, *logos* in Greek means not only "meaning" but also "spirit." Spiritual issues such as man's aspiration for a meaningful existence as well as the frustration of this aspiration, are both dealt with by logotherapy in *spiritual* terms. They are taken sincerely and earnestly instead of being traced back to unconscious roots and sources, thus being dealt with merely in *instinctual* terms.

Whenever a doctor fails to distinguish between the spiritual dimension as against the instinctual, a dangerous confusion may arise. Let me quote the following instance: A high-ranking American diplomat came to my office in Vienna in order to continue psychoanalytic treatment which he had begun five years previously with an analyst in New York. At the outset I asked him why he thought he should be analyzed, why his analysis had been started in the first place. It turned out that the patient was discontented with his career and found it most difficult to

comply with American foreign policy. His analyst, however, had told him again and again that he should try to
reconcile himself with his father; because the government
of the U. S. as well as his superiors were "nothing but"
father images and, consequently, his dissatisfaction with
his job was due to the hatred he unconsciously harbored
toward his father. Through an analysis lasting five years,
the patient had been prompted more and more to accept
his analyst's interpretations until he finally was unable to
see the forest of reality for the trees of symbols and
images. After a few interviews, it was clear that his
will to meaning was frustrated by his vocation, and he
actually longed to be engaged in some other kind of work.
As there was no reason for not giving up his profession
and embarking on a different one, he did so, with most
gratifying results. He has remained contented in this
new occupation for over five years, as he recently reported.
I doubt that, in this case, I was dealing with a neurotic
condition at all, and that is why I thought that he did not
need any psychotherapy, nor even logotherapy, for the
simple reason that he was not actually a patient. Not every
conflict is necessarily neurotic; some amount of conflict is
normal and healthy. In a similar sense suffering is not
always a pathological phenomenon; rather than being a
symptom of neurosis, suffering may well be a human
achievement, especially if the suffering grows out of existential frustration. I would strictly deny that one's search
for a meaning to his existence, or even his doubt of it,
in every case is derived from, or results in, any disease.
Existential frustration is in itself neither pathological nor
pathogenic. A man's concern, even his despair, over the
worthwhileness of life is a *spiritual distress* but by no

means a *mental disease*. It may well be that interpreting the first in terms of the latter motivates a doctor to bury his patient's existential despair under a heap of tranquilizing drugs. It is his task, rather, to pilot the patient through his existential crises of growth and development.

Logotherapy regards its assignment as that of assisting the patient to find meaning in his life. Inasmuch as logotherapy makes him aware of the hidden *logos* of his existence, it is an analytical process. To this extent, logotherapy resembles psychoanalysis. However, in logotherapy's attempt to make something conscious again it does not restrict its activity to *instinctual* facts within the individual's unconscious but also cares for *spiritual* realities such as the potential meaning of his existence to be fulfilled, as well as his *will* to meaning. Any analysis, however, even when it refrains from including the noölogical or spiritual dimension in its therapeutic process, tries to make the patient aware of what he actually longs for in the depth of his being. Logotherapy deviates from psychoanalysis insofar as it considers man as a being whose main concern consists in fulfilling a meaning and in actualizing values, rather than in the mere gratification and satisfaction of drives and instincts, or in merely reconciling the conflicting claims of id, ego and superego, or in the mere adaptation and adjustment to society and environment.

Noö-dynamics

To be sure, man's search for meaning and values may arouse inner tension rather than inner equilibrium. However, precisely such tension is an indispensable prerequisite of mental health. There is nothing in the world, I venture to say, that would so effectively help one to survive even the worst conditions, as the knowledge that there is a meaning in one's life. There is much wisdom in the words of Nietzsche: "He who has a *why* to live for can bear almost any *how*." I can see in these words a motto which holds true for any psychotherapy. In the Nazi concentration camps, one could have witnessed (and this was later confirmed by American psychiatrists both in Japan and Korea) that those who knew that there was a task waiting for them to fulfill were most apt to survive.

As for myself, when I was taken to the concentration camp of Auschwitz, a manuscript of mine ready for publication was confiscated.[1] Certainly, my deep concern to write this manuscript anew helped me to survive the rigors of the camp. For instance, when I fell ill with typhus fever I jotted down on little scraps of paper many notes intended to enable me to rewrite the manuscript, should I live to the day of liberation. I am sure that this reconstruction of my lost manuscript in the dark barracks of a Bavarian concentration camp assisted me in overcoming the danger of collapse.

Thus it can be seen that mental health is based on a certain degree of tension, the tension between what one has already achieved and what one still ought to accomplish, or the gap between what one is and what one should become. Such a tension is inherent in the human being and therefore is indispensable to mental well-being. We should not, then, be hesitant about challenging man with a

---

[1] It was the first version of my first book, the English translation of which was published by Alfred A. Knopf, New York, in 1955, under the title *The Doctor and the Soul: An Introduction to Logotherapy.*

potential meaning for him to fulfill. It is only thus that
we evoke his will to meaning from its state of latency. I
consider it a dangerous misconception of mental hygiene
to assume that what man needs in the first place is equilibrium or, as it is called in biology, "homeostasis," i.e., a
tension-less state. What man actually needs is not a tension-
less state but rather the striving and struggling for some
goal worthy of him. What he needs is not the discharge
of tension at any cost, but the call of a potential meaning
waiting to be fulfilled by him. What man needs is not
homeostasis but what I call "noö-dynamics," i.e., the spiritual dynamics in a polar field of tension where one pole is
represented by a meaning to be fulfilled and the other pole
by the man who must fulfill it. And one should not think
that this holds true only for normal conditions; in neurotic
individuals, it is even more valid. If architects want to
strengthen a decrepit arch, they *increase* the load which
is laid upon it, for thereby the parts are joined more firmly
together. So if therapists wish to foster their patients'
mental health, they should not be afraid to increase that
load through a reorientation toward the meaning of one's
life.

After having shown the beneficial impact of meaning
orientation, I turn to the detrimental influence of that
feeling of which so many patients complain today, namely,
the feeling of the total and ultimate meaninglessness of
their lives. They lack the awareness of a meaning worth
living for. They are haunted by the experience of their
inner emptiness, a void within themselves; they are caught
in that situation which I have called the "existential
vacuum."

The Existential Vacuum

The existential vacuum is a widespread phenomenon of the twentieth century. This is understandable; it may be due to a two-fold loss which man had to undergo since he became a truly human being. At the beginning of human history, man lost some of the basic animal instincts in which an animal's behavior is imbedded and by which it is secured. Such security, like Paradise, is closed to man forever; man has to make choices. In addition to this, however, man has suffered another loss in his more recent development inasmuch as the traditions which buttressed his behavior are now rapidly diminishing. No instinct tells him what he has to do, and no tradition tells him what he ought to do; sometimes he does not even know what he wishes to do. Instead, he either wishes to do what other people do (conformism) or he does what other people wish him to do (totalitarianism).

A cross-sectional, statistical survey of the patients and the nursing staff was conducted by my staff in the neurological department of the Vienna Poliklinik Hospital. It revealed that 55 per cent of the persons questioned showed a more or less marked degree of existential vacuum. In other words, more than half of them had experienced a loss of the feeling that life is meaningful.

This existential vacuum manifests itself mainly in a state of boredom. Now we can understand Schopenhauer when he said that mankind was apparently doomed to vacillate eternally between the two extremes of distress and boredom. In actual fact, boredom is now causing, and certainly bringing to psychiatrists, more problems to solve than distress. And these problems are growing increasingly crucial, for progressive automation will probably lead to an enormous increase in the leisure hours for the average worker. The pity of it is many of these will not know what to do with all their newly acquired free time.

Let us think, for instance, of "Sunday neurosis," that kind of depression which afflicts people who become aware of the lack of content in their lives when the rush of the busy week is over and the void within themselves becomes manifest. Not a few cases of suicide can be traced back to this existential vacuum. Such widespread phenomena as alcoholism and juvenile delinquency would not be understandable unless we recognize the existential vacuum underlying them. This is also true of the crises of pensioners and aging people.

Moreover, there are various masks and guises under which the existential vacuum appears. Sometimes the frustrated will to meaning is vicariously compensated for by a will to power, including the most primitive form of the will to power, the will to money. In other cases, the place of frustrated will to meaning is taken by the will to pleasure. That is why existential frustration often eventuates in sexual compensation. We can observe in such cases, that the sexual libido becomes rampant in the existential vacuum.

An analogous event occurs in neurotic cases. There are certain types of feed-back mechanisms and vicious circle formations which I will touch upon later. One can observe again and again, however, that this symptomatology has invaded an existential vacuum wherein it then continues to flourish. In such patients, what we have to deal with is not a noögenic neurosis. However, we will never succeed in having the patient overcome his condition, if we have not supplemented the psychotherapeutic treatment with logo-therapy. For by filling the existential vacuum, the patient will be prevented from further relapses. Therefore, logo-therapy is indicated not only in noögenic cases, as pointed out above, but also in psychogenic cases, and sometimes even the somatogenic (pseudo-) neuroses. Viewed in this light, a statement once made by Magda B. Arnold[2] is justi-fied: "Every therapy must in some way, no matter how re-stricted, also be logotherapy."

Let us now consider what we can do if a patient asks what *is* the meaning of his life.

The Meaning of Life

I doubt whether a doctor can answer this question in general terms. For the meaning of life differs from man to man, from day to day and from hour to hour. What matters, therefore, is not the meaning of life in general but rather the specific meaning of a person's life at a given mo-ment. To put the question in general terms would be com-parable to the question posed to a chess champion, "Tell me, Master, what is the best move in the world?" There simply is no such thing as the best or even a good move apart from a particular situation in a game and the par-ticular personality of one's opponent. The same holds for human existence. One should not search for an abstract meaning of life. Everyone has his own specific vocation or mission in life to carry out a concrete assignment which demands fulfillment. Therein he cannot be replaced, nor

[2] Magda B. Arnold and John A. Gasson, *The Human Person*, Ronald Press, New York, 1954, p. 618.

can his life be repeated. Thus, everyone's task is as unique as is his specific opportunity to implement it.

Freedom is not the last word. Freedom is only part of the story and half of the truth. Freedom is but the negative aspect of the whole phenomenon whose positive aspect is responsibleness. In fact, freedom is in danger of degenerating into mere arbitrariness unless it is lived in terms of responsibleness. That is why *I recommend that the Statue of Liberty on the East Coast be supplemented by a Statue of Responsibility on the West Coast.*

As each situation in life represents a challenge to man and presents a problem for him to solve, the question of the meaning of life may actually be reversed. Ultimately, man should not ask what the meaning of his life is, but rather he must recognize that it is *he* who is asked. In a word, each man is questioned by life; and he can only answer to life by *answering for* his own life; to life he can only respond by being responsible. Thus, logotherapy sees in responsibleness the very essence of human existence.

The Essence of Existence

This emphasis on responsibleness is reflected in the categorical imperative of logotherapy, which is: "So live as if you were living already for the second time and as if you had acted the first time as wrongly as you are about to act now!" It seems to me that there is nothing which would stimulate a man's sense of responsibleness more than this maxim, which invites him to imagine first that the present is past and, second, that the past may yet be changed and amended. Such a precept confronts him with life's *finiteness* as well as the *finality* of what he makes out of both his life and himself.

Logotherapy tries to make the patient fully aware of his own responsibleness; and therefore it must leave to him the option for what, to what or to whom, he understands himself to be responsible. That is why a logotherapist is the least tempted of all psychotherapists to impose value judgments on the patients, for he will never permit the patient to pass to the doctor the responsibility of judging.

It is, therefore, up to the patient to decide whether he should interpret his life task as being responsible to society or to his own conscience. The majority, however, consider themselves accountable before God; they represent those who do not interpret their own lives merely in terms of a task assigned to them but also in terms of the task-master who has assigned it to them.

Logotherapy is neither teaching nor preaching. It is as far removed from logical reasoning as it is from moral exhortation. To put it figuratively, the role played by a logotherapist is rather that of an eye specialist than of a painter. A painter tries to convey to us a picture of the world as he sees it, an ophthalmologist tries to enable us to see the world as it really is. The logotherapist's role consists in widening and broadening the visual field of the patient so that the whole spectrum of meaning and values becomes conscious and visible to him. Logotherapy does not need to impose any judgments on the patient; for, actually, truth imposes itself and needs no intervention.

By declaring that man is a responsible creature and must actualize the potential meaning of his life, I wish to stress that the true meaning of life is to be found in the world rather than within man or his own psyche, as though it were a closed system. By the same token, the real aim of human existence cannot be found in what is called self-actualization. Human existence is essentially self-transcendence rather than self-actualization. Self-actualization is not a possible aim at all; for the simple reason that the more a man would strive for it, the more he would miss it. For only to the extent to which man commits himself to the fulfillment of his life's meaning, to this extent he also actualizes himself. In other words, self-actualization cannot be attained if it is made an end in itself, but only as a side-effect of self-transcendence.

We have shown that the meaning of life always changes. But it never ceases to exist. According to logotherapy, we can discover this meaning in life in three different ways: (1) by doing a deed, (2) by experiencing a value, (3) by suffering. The first, the way of achievement or accomplishment, is quite obvious. The second and third need further elaboration.

The second way of finding a meaning in life is by experiencing something, such as a work of nature or culture; and also by experiencing someone, i.e., by love.

The Meaning of Love

Love is the only way to grasp another human being in the innermost core of his personality. No one can become fully aware of the very essence of another human being unless he loves him. By the spiritual act of love he is enabled to see the essential traits and features in the beloved person; and even more, he sees that which is potential in him; which is not yet actualized but yet ought to be actualized. Furthermore, by his love, the loving person enables the beloved person to actualize these potentialities. By making him aware of what he can be and of what he should become, he makes these potentialities come true.

In logotherapy, love is not interpreted as a mere epi-phenomenon[3] of sexual drives and instincts in the sense of a so-called sublimation. Love is as primary a phenomenon as sex. Normally, sex is a mode of expression for love. Sex is justified, even sanctified, as soon as, but only as long as, it is a vehicle of love. Thus love is not understood as a mere side-effect of sex but a way of expressing the experience of that ultimate togetherness which is called love.

A third way to find a meaning in life is by suffering.

The Meaning of Suffering

Whenever one is confronted with an inescapable, un-avoidable situation, whenever one has to face a fate which cannot be changed, e.g., an incurable disease, such as an inoperable cancer; just then one is given a last chance to actualize the highest value, to fulfill the deepest meaning, the meaning of suffering. For what matters above all is the attitude we take toward suffering, the attitude in which we take our suffering upon ourselves.

Let me cite a clear-cut example: Once, an elderly general practitioner consulted me because of his severe depression. He could not overcome the loss of his wife who had died two years before and whom he had loved above all else. Now how could I help him? What should I tell him? Well, I refrained from telling him anything but instead confronted him with the question, "What would have

[3] A phenomenon that occurs as the result of a primary phenomenon.

happened, Doctor, if you had died first, and your wife would have had to survive you?" "Oh," he said, "for her this would have been terrible; how she would have suffered!" Whereupon I replied, "You see, Doctor, such a suffering has been spared her, and it was you who have spared her this suffering; but now, you have to pay for it by surviving and mourning her." He said no word but shook my hand and calmly left my office. Suffering ceases to be suffering in some way at the moment it finds a meaning, such as the meaning of a sacrifice.

Of course, this was no therapy in the proper sense since, first, his despair was no disease; and second, I could not change his fate, I could not revive his wife. But in that moment I did succeed in changing his *attitude* toward his unalterable fate inasmuch as from that time on he could at least see a meaning in his suffering. It is one of the basic tenets of logotherapy that man's main concern is not to gain pleasure or to avoid pain but rather to see a meaning in his life. That is why man is even ready to suffer, on the condition, to be sure, that his suffering has a meaning.

It goes without saying that suffering would not have a meaning unless it were absolutely necessary; e.g., a cancer which can be cured by surgery must not be shouldered by the patient as though it were his cross. This would be masochism rather than heroism.

Traditional psychotherapy has aimed at restoring one's capacity to work and to enjoy life; logotherapy includes these, yet goes further by having the patient regain his capacity to suffer, if need be, thereby finding meaning even in suffering. In this context Edith Wiesskopf-Joelson, professor of psychology at the University of Georgia, contends, in her article on logotherapy,[4] that "our current mental-hygiene philosophy stresses the idea that people ought to be happy, that unhappiness is a symptom of maladjustment. Such a value system might be responsible for the fact that the burden of unavoidable unhappiness is increased by unhappiness about being unhappy." And in another paper[5] she expresses the hope that logotherapy "may help counteract certain unhealthy trends in the present-day culture of the United States, where the incurable sufferer is given very little opportunity to be proud of his suffering and to consider it ennobling rather than degrading" so that "he is not only unhappy, but also ashamed of being unhappy."

There are situations in which one is cut off from the opportunity to do one's work or to enjoy one's life; but what never can be ruled out is the unavoidability of suffering. In accepting this challenge to suffer bravely, life has a meaning up to the last moment, and it retains this meaning literally to the end. In other words, life's meaning is an unconditional one for it even includes the potential meaning of suffering.

Let me recall that which was perhaps the deepest experience I had in the concentration camp. The odds of surviving the camp were no more than 1 to 28, as can easily be verified by exact statistics. It did not even seem possible, let alone probable, that the manuscript of my first book which I had hidden in my coat when I arrived at Auschwitz, would ever be rescued. Thus, I had to undergo and to overcome the loss of my spiritual child. And now it seemed as if nothing and no one would survive me; neither a

4 "Some Comments on a Viennese School of Psychiatry," *The Journal of Abnormal and Social Psychology*, 51, 701–703, 1955.
5 "Logotherapy and Existential Analysis," *Acta psychotherap.*, 6, 193–204, 1958.

physical nor a spiritual child of my own! So I found myself confronted with the question whether under such circumstances my life was ultimately void of any meaning.

Not yet did I notice that an answer to this question with which I was wrestling so passionately was already in store for me, and that soon thereafter this answer would be given to me. This was the case when I had to surrender my clothes and in turn inherited the worn-out rags of an inmate who had already been sent to the gas chamber immediately after his arrival at the Auschwitz railway station. Instead of the many pages of my manuscript, I found in a pocket of the newly acquired coat one single page torn out of a Hebrew prayer book, containing the main Jewish prayer, *Shema Yisrael.* How should I have interpreted such a "coincidence" other than as a challenge to *live* my thoughts instead of merely putting them on paper?

A bit later, I remember, it seemed to me that I would die in the near future. In this critical situation, however, my concern was different from that of most of my comrades. Their question was, "Will we survive the camp? For, if not, all this suffering has no meaning." The question which beset me was, "Has all this suffering, this dying around us, a meaning? For, if not, then ultimately there is no meaning to survival; for a life whose meaning depends upon such a happenstance—as whether one escapes or not—ultimately would not be worth living at all."

Meta-clinical Problems

More and more, a doctor is confronted with the questions, What is life? What is suffering after all? Indeed, incessantly and continually a psychiatrist is approached today by patients who confront him with human problems rather than neurotic symptoms. Some of the people who nowadays call on a psychiatrist would have seen a pastor, priest or rabbi in former days, but now they often refuse to be handed over to a clergyman, so that the doctor is confronted with philosophical questions rather than emotional conflicts.

A *Logodrama*

I should like to cite the following instance: Once, the mother of a boy who had died at the age of eleven years was admitted to my clinic after a suicide attempt. My associate, Dr. Kocourek, invited her to join a therapeutic group, and it happened that I stepped into the room of the clinic where he was conducting a psychodrama. She was telling her story. At the death of her boy she was left alone with another, older son, who was crippled, suffering from infantile paralysis. The poor boy had to be moved around in a chair. His mother, however, rebelled against her fate. But when she tried to commit suicide together with him, it was the crippled son who prevented her from doing so; he liked living! For him, life had remained meaningful. Why was it not so for his mother? How could her life still have a meaning? And how could we help her to become aware of it?

Improvising, I participated in the discussion, and questioned another woman in the group. I asked her how old she was and she answered, "Thirty." I replied, "No, you are not thirty but instead eighty and lying on your deathbed. And now you are looking back on your life, a life which was childless but full of financial success and social prestige." And then I invited her to imagine what she would feel in this situation. "What will you think of it? What will you say to yourself?" Let me quote what she actually said from a tape which was recorded during that session. "Oh, I married a millionaire; I had an easy life full of wealth; and I lived it up! I flirted with men, I teased them! But now, I am eighty; I have no children of my own. Looking back as an old woman, I cannot see what all that was for; actually, I must say, my life was a failure!"

I then invited the mother of the handicapped son to imagine herself similarly looking back over *her* life. Let us listen to what she had to say as recorded on the tape: "I wished to have children and this wish has been granted to me; one boy died; the other, however, the crippled one, would have been sent to an institution if I had not taken over his care. Though he is crippled and helpless, he is after all my boy. And so I have made a fuller life possible for him; I have made a better human being out of my son." At this moment, there was an outburst of tears, and crying, she continued: "As for myself, I can look back peacefully on my life; for I can say my life was full of meaning, and I have tried hard to fulfill it; I have done my best—I have done the best for my son. My life was no failure!" Viewing her life as if from her deathbed, she had suddenly been able to see a meaning in it, a meaning which included even all of her sufferings. By the same token, however, it had become clear as well that a life of short duration, like that, for example, of her dead boy, could be so rich in joy and love, that it could contain more meaning than a life lasting eighty years.

After a while I proceeded to another question, this time addressing myself to the whole group. The question was whether an ape which was being used to develop poliomyelitis serum, and for this reason punctured again and again, would ever be able to grasp the meaning of its suffering. Unanimously, the group replied of course it would not; for with its limited intelligence, it could not enter into the world of man, i.e., the only world in which its suffering would be understandable. Then I pushed forward with the following question: "And what about man? Are you sure that the human world is a terminal point in the evolution of the cosmos? Is it not conceivable that there is still another dimension possible, a world beyond man's world; a world in which the question of an ultimate meaning of human suffering would find an answer?"

The Supra-meaning

This ultimate meaning necessarily exceeds and surpasses the finite intellectual capacities of man; in logotherapy, we speak in this context of a supra-meaning. What is demanded of man is not, as some existential philosophers teach, to endure the meaninglessness of life; but rather to bear his incapacity to grasp its unconditional meaningfulness in rational terms. *Logos* is deeper than logic.

A psychiatrist who goes beyond the concept of the supra-meaning, would sooner or later be embarrassed by his patients just as I was when my daughter at about six years of age asked me the question, "Why do we speak of the *good* Lord?" Whereupon I said, "Some weeks ago, you were suffering from measles, and then, the *good* Lord sent you full recovery." However, the little girl was not content but she retorted, "Well; but, please, Daddy, do not forget: in the first place, he had sent me the measles."

However, when a patient stands on the firm ground of religious belief, there can be no objection to making use of the therapeutic effect of his religious convictions and thereby drawing upon his spiritual resources. In order to do so, the psychiatrist may put himself in the place of the patient. That is exactly what I did once, for instance, when a rabbi from Eastern Europe turned to me and told me his story. He had lost his first wife and their six children in the concentration camp of Auschwitz where they were gassed, and now, it turned out that his second wife was sterile. I observed that procreation is not the only meaning of life, for then life in itself would become meaningless, and something which in itself is meaningless cannot be rendered meaningful merely by its perpetuation. However, the rabbi evaluated his plight as an orthodox Jew in terms of despair that there was no son of his own who would ever say Kaddish[6] for him after his death.

But I would not give up. I made a last attempt to help him by inquiring whether he did not hope to see his children again in Heaven. However, my question was followed by an outburst of tears, and now the true reason of his despair came to the fore: he explained that his children, since they died as innocent martyrs,[7] were thus found worthy of the highest place in Heaven, but as for himself he could not expect, as an old sinful man, to be assigned

[6] A prayer for the dead.
[7] *Lkiddush hashem,* i.e., for the sanctification of God's name.

the same place. I did not give up but retorted, "Is it not conceivable, Rabbi, that precisely this was the meaning of your surviving your children; that you may be purified through these years of suffering, so that finally you, too, though not innocent like your children, may *become* worthy of joining them in Heaven? Is it not written in the Psalms that God preserves all your tears?[8] So, perhaps none of your sufferings were in vain." For the first time in many years he found relief from his suffering through the new point of view which I was able to open up to him.

Life's Transitoriness

To those things which seem to take meaning away from human life belong not only suffering but dying as well, not only distress but also death. I never tire of saying that the only really transitory aspects of life are the potentialities; but as soon as they are actualized, they are rendered realities at that very moment; they are saved and delivered into the past, wherein they are rescued and preserved from transitoriness. For, in the past, nothing is irrecoverably lost but everything irrevocably stored.

Thus, the transitoriness of our existence in no way makes it meaningless. But it does constitute our responsibleness; for everything hinges upon our realizing the essentially transitory possibilities. Man constantly makes his choice concerning the mass of present potentialities; which of these will be condemned to non-being and which will be actualized? Which choice made an actuality once and for-

---

[8] "Thou hast kept count of my tossings; put thou my tears in thy bottle! Are they not in thy book?" (Ps. 56, 8.)

ever, an immortal "footprint in the sands of time"? At any moment, man must decide, for better or for worse, what will be the monument of his existence.

Usually, to be sure, man considers only the stubble field of transitoriness and overlooks the full granaries of the past, wherein he had salvaged once and for all his deeds his joys and also his sufferings. Nothing can be undone, and nothing can be done away with. I should say *having been* is the surest kind of being.

Logotherapy, keeping in mind the essential transitoriness of human existence, is not pessimistic but rather activistic. To express this point figuratively we might say: The pessimist resembles a man who observes with fear and sadness that his wall calendar, from which he daily tears a sheet, grows thinner with each passing day. On the other hand, the person who attacks the problems of life actively is like a man who removes each successive leaf from his calendar and files it neatly and carefully away with its predecessors, after first having jotted down a few diary notes on the back. He can reflect with pride and joy on all the richness set down in these notes, on all the life he has already lived to the full. What will it matter to him if he notices that he is growing old? Has he any reason to envy the young people whom he sees, or wax nostalgic over his own lost youth? What reasons has he to envy a young person? For the possibilities that a young person has, the future which is in store for him? "No, thank you," he will think. "Instead of possibilities, I have realities in my past, not only the reality of work done, and of love loved but of sufferings bravely suffered. These sufferings are even the things of which I am most proud, though these are things which cannot inspire envy."

Logotherapy as a Technique

A realistic fear, like the fear of death, cannot be tranquilized away by its psychodynamic interpretation; on the other hand, a neurotic fear, such as agoraphobia, cannot be cured by philosophical understanding. However, logotherapy has developed a special technique to handle such cases, too. To understand what is going on whenever this technique is used, we take as a starting point a condition which is frequently met in neurotic individuals, namely, anticipatory anxiety. It is characteristic of this fear that it produces precisely that of which the patient is afraid. An individual, for example, who is afraid of blushing when he enters a large room and faces many people, will actually blush. In this context, one might transpose the saying "the wish is father to the thought" to "the fear is mother of the event."

Ironically enough, in the same way that fear brings to pass what one is afraid of, likewise a forced intention makes impossible what one forcibly wishes. This excessive intention, or "hyper-intention" as I should call it, can be observed particularly in cases of sexual neurosis. The more a man tries to demonstrate his sexual potency or a woman her ability to experience orgasm, the less they are able to succeed. Pleasure is, and must remain, a side-effect or by-product, and is destroyed and spoiled to the degree to which it is made a goal in itself.

In addition to excessive intention as described above, excessive attention or "hyper-reflection" as it is called in logotherapy, may also be pathogenic (that is lead to sickness). The following clinical report will indicate what I mean: A young woman came to me complaining of being frigid. The case history showed that in her childhood she had been sexually abused by her father. However, it had not been this traumatic experience in itself which had eventuated in her sexual neurosis, as could easily be evidenced. For it turned out that, through reading popular psychoanalytic literature, the patient had lived all the time in the fearful expectation of the toll which her traumatic experience would some day take. This anticipatory anxiety resulted both in excessive intention to confirm her femininity, as well as the excessive attention centered upon herself rather than upon her partner. This was enough to incapacitate the patient for the peak experience of sexual pleasure since the orgasm is made an object of intention, and an object of attention as well, instead of remaining an unintended effect of unreflected dedication and devotion to the partner. After undergoing short-term logotherapy, the patient's excessive attention and intention of her ability to experience orgasm had been "dereflected," to introduce another logotherapeutic term. When her attention was refocused toward the proper object, i.e., the partner, orgasm established itself spontaneously.[9]

On the two-fold fact that fear makes come true that which one is afraid of, and that hyper-intention makes impossible what one wishes, logotherapy bases its technique called "paradoxical intention." In German I described it as early as 1939 (Viktor E. Frankl, "Zur medikamentösen

---

[9] In order to treat cases of sexual impotence, in logotherapy a specific technique has been developed, based on its theory of hyper-intention and hyper-reflection as sketched above (Viktor E. Frankl, "The Pleasure Principle and Sexual Neurosis," *The International Journal of Sexology*, Vol. 5, Nr. 3, pp. 128-30 [1952]). Of course, this cannot be dealt with in this brief presentation of the principles of logotherapy.

Unterstützung der Psychotherapie bei Neurosen," *Schwei-zer Archiv für Neurologie und Psychiatrie,* Vol. 43, pp. 26–31). In this approach the phobic patient is invited to intend, even if only for a moment, precisely that which he fears.

Let me recall a case. A young physician consulted me because of his fear of perspiring. Whenever he expected an outbreak of perspiration, this anticipatory anxiety was enough to precipitate excessive sweating. In order to cut this circle formation I advised the patient, in the event that sweating should recur, to resolve deliberately to show people how much he could sweat. A week later he returned to report that whenever he met anyone who triggered his anticipatory anxiety, he said to himself, "I only sweated out a quart before, but now I'm going to pour at least ten quarts!" The result was that, after suffering from his phobia for four years, he was able, after a single session, to free himself permanently of it within one week.

The reader will note that this procedure consists in a reversal of the patient's attitude, inasmuch as his fear is replaced by a paradoxical wish. By this treatment, the wind is taken out of the sails of the anxiety.

Such a procedure, however, must make use of the specifically human capacity for self-detachment inherent in a sense of humor. This basic capacity to detach one from oneself is actualized whenever the logotherapeutic tech-nique called "paradoxical intention" is applied. At the same time, the patient is enabled to put himself at a distance from his own neurosis. A statement consistent with this is found in Gordon W. Allport's book, *The Individual and His Religion* (New York: The Macmillan Co., 1956, p. 92): "The neurotic who learns to laugh at himself may be on the way to self-management, perhaps to cure." Paradoxical intention is the empirical validation and clinical application of Allport's statement.

A few more case reports may serve to clarify this method further. The following patient was a bookkeeper who had been treated by many doctors and in several clinics without any therapeutic success. When he came to my clinic, he was in extreme despair, admitting that he was close to suicide. For some years, he had suffered from a writer's cramp which had recently become so severe that he was in danger of losing his job. Therefore only immediate short-term therapy could alleviate the situation. In starting treatment my associate recommended to the patient that he do just the opposite from what he usually had done; namely, instead of trying to write as neatly and legibly as possible, to write with the worst possible scrawl. He was advised to say to himself, "Now I will show people what a good scribbler I am!" And at the moment in which he deliberately tried to scribble, he was unable to do so. "I tried to scrawl but simply could not do it," he said the next day. Within forty-eight hours the patient was in this way freed from his writer's cramp, and remained free for the observation period after he had been treated. He is a happy man again and fully able to work.

A similar case, dealing, however, with speaking rather than writing, was related to me by a colleague in the Laryngological Department of the Poliklinik Hospital. It was the most severe case of stuttering he had met in his many years of practice. Never in his life, as far as the stutterer could remember, had he been free from his speech trouble, even for a moment, except once. This happened when he was twelve years old and had hooked a ride on a streetcar. When caught by the conductor, he thought that the only way to escape would be to elicit his sympathy, and so he tried to demonstrate that he was just a poor stuttering boy. At that moment, in which he tried to stutter, he was unable to do it. Without meaning to, he had practiced paradoxical intention, though not for therapeutic purposes.

However, this presentation should not leave the impression that paradoxical intention is effective only in monosymptomatic cases. By means of this logotherapeutic technique, my collaborators at the Vienna Poliklinik Hospital have succeeded in bringing relief even in obsessive-compulsive character neuroses of a most severe degree and duration. I refer, for instance, to a woman sixty-five years of age who had suffered for sixty years from a washing compulsion of such severity that I expected a lobotomy to be the only available procedure for bringing relief. However, my associate started logotherapeutic treatment by means of paradoxical intention, and two months later the patient was able to lead a normal life. Before admission to the clinic, she had confessed, "Life was hell for me." Handicapped by her compulsion and bacterio-phobic obsession, she finally remained in bed all day unable to do any housework. It would not be accurate to say that she is now completely free of symptoms, for an obsession may come to her mind. However, she is able to "joke about it," as she says; in short, to apply paradoxical intention.

Paradoxical intention can also be applied in cases of sleep disturbance. The fear of sleeplessness[10] results in a hyper-intention to fall asleep, which, in turn, incapacitates

---

[10] The fear of sleeplessness is, in the majority of cases, due to the patient's ignorance of the fact that the organism provides itself *by itself* with the minimum amount of sleep really needed.

the patient to do so. To overcome this particular fear, I usually advise the patient not to try to sleep but rather to try to do just the opposite, that is, to stay awake as long as possible. In other words, the hyper-intention to fall asleep arising from the anticipatory anxiety of not being able to do so, must be replaced by the paradoxical intention not to fall asleep, which soon will be followed by sleep.

Paradoxical intention is no panacea. Yet it lends itself as a useful tool in treating obsessive-compulsive and phobic conditions, especially in cases with underlying anticipatory anxiety. Moreover it is a short-term therapeutic device. However, one should not conclude that such a short-term therapy necessarily results in only temporary therapeutic effects. One of "the more common illusions of Freudian orthodoxy," to quote the late Emil A. Gutheil[11], "is that the durability of results corresponds to the length of therapy." In my files there is, for instance, the case report of a patient to whom paradoxical intention was administered more than twenty years ago; the therapeutic effect proved to be, nevertheless, a permanent one.

One of the most remarkable facts is that paradoxical intention is effective irrespective of the etiological basis in the case concerned. This confirms a statement once made by Edith Weisskopf-Joelson:[12] "Although traditional psychotherapy has insisted that therapeutic practices have to be based on findings on etiology, it is possible that certain factors might cause neuroses during early childhood and that entirely different factors might relieve neuroses during adulthood."

[11] *American Journal of Psychotherapy,* 10: 134, 1956.
[12] "Some Comments on a Viennese School of Psychiatry," *The Journal of Abnormal and Social Psychology,* 51: 701-703, 1955.

What is so often regarded as a cause of neurosis, i.e., complexes, conflicts and traumata, is sometimes rather a symptom of the neurosis than its cause. A reef which appears at low tide is certainly not the cause of low tide; but it is rather low tide which causes the reef to appear. Now, what is *melancholia* if not some sort of emotional low tide? Again, the guilt feelings which are so typically displayed in "endogenous depressions" (which must not be confounded with neurotic ones!) are not the cause of this special type of depression; but rather the reverse is true inasmuch as this emotional low tide makes those guilt feelings appear at the surface of consciousness; it only brings them to the fore.

As for the actual causation of neuroses, apart from constitutional elements, whether somatic or psychic in nature, such feedback mechanisms as anticipatory anxiety seem to be a major pathogenic factor. A given symptom is responded to by a phobia, the phobia triggers the symptom, and the symptom, in turn, reinforces the phobia. A similar chain of events, however, can be observed in obsessive-compulsive cases in which the patient fights the ideas which haunt him.[13] Thereby, however, he increases their power to disturb him, since pressure precipitates counter-pressure. Again the symptom is reinforced! On the other hand, as soon as the patient stops fighting his obsessions and instead tries to ridicule them by dealing with them in an ironical way, by applying paradoxical intention, *the vicious circle is cut,* the symptom diminishes and finally atrophies. In the fortunate case where there is no existential vacuum

---

[13] This is often motivated by the patient's fear that his obsessions indicate an imminent or even actual psychosis; the patient is not aware of the empirical fact that an obsessive-compulsive neurosis is immunizing him against a formal psychosis, rather than endangering him in this direction.

which invites and elicits the symptom, the patient will not only succeed in ridiculing his neurotic fear but finally will succeed in completely ignoring it.

As we see, anticipatory anxiety has to be counteracted by paradoxical intention; hyper-intention as well as hyper-reflection have to be counteracted by de-reflection; de-reflection, however, ultimately is not possible except by the patient's orientation toward his specific vocation and mission in life.[14]

It is not the neurotic's self-concern, whether pity or contempt, which breaks the circle formation; the cue to cure is self-transcendence!

The Collective Neurosis

Every age has its own collective neurosis, and every age needs its own psychotherapy to cope with it. The existential vacuum which is the mass neurosis of the present time, can be described as a private and personal form of nihilism; for nihilism can be defined as the contention that being has no meaning. As for psychotherapy, however, it will never be able to cope with this state of affairs on a mass scale if it does not keep itself free from the impact and influence of the contemporary trends of a nihilistic philosophy; otherwise it represents a symptom of the mass neurosis rather than its possible cure. Psychotherapy would not only reflect a nihilistic philosophy but also, even though unwillingly and unwittingly, transmit to the patient what is actually a caricature rather than a true picture of man.

[14] This conviction is supported by Allport who once said: "As the focus of striving shifts from the conflict to selfless goals, the life as a whole becomes sounder even though the neurosis may never completely disappear" (l. c., p. 95).

First of all, there is a danger inherent in the teaching of man's "nothingbutness," the theory that man is nothing but the result of biological, psychological and sociological conditions, or the product of heredity and environment. Such a view of man makes him into a robot, not a human being. This neurotic fatalism is fostered and strengthened by a psychotherapy which denies that man is free.

To be sure, a human being is a finite thing, and his freedom is restricted. It is not freedom from conditions but it is freedom to take a stand toward the conditions. As I once ("Value Dimensions in Teaching," a color television film produced by Hollywood Animators, Inc., for the California Junior College Association) put it: As a professor in two fields, neurology and psychiatry, I am fully aware of the extent to which man is subject to biological, psychological and sociological conditions. But in addition to being a professor in two fields I am a survivor of four camps—concentration camps, that is, and as such I also bear witness to the unexpected extent to which man is capable of defying and braving even the worst conditions conceivable.

Critique of Pan-determinism

Psychoanalysis has often been blamed for its so-called pan-sexualism. I, for one, doubt whether this reproach has ever been legitimate. However, there is something which seems to me to be an even more erroneous and dangerous assumption, namely, that which I call "pan-determinism." By that I mean the view of man which disregards his capacity to take a stand toward any conditions whatsoever. Man is *not* fully conditioned and determined but rather determines himself whether he gives in to conditions or stands up to them. In other words, man is ultimately self-determining. Man does not simply exist but always decides what his existence will be, what he will become in the next moment.

By the same token, every human being has the freedom to change at any instant. Therefore, we can predict his future only within the large frame of a statistical survey referring to a whole group; the individual personality, however, remains essentially unpredictable. The basis for any predictions would be represented by biological, psychological or sociological conditions. Yet one of the main features of human existence is the capacity to rise above such conditions and transcend them. In the same manner, man ultimately transcends himself; a human being is a self-transcending being.

Let me cite the case of Dr. J. He was the only man I ever encountered in my whole life whom I would dare to call a Mephistophelean being, a satanic figure. At that time he was generally called "the mass murderer of Steinhof," the name of the large mental hospital in Vienna. When the Nazis started their euthanasia program, he held all the strings in his hands and was so fanatic in the job assigned to him that he tried not to let one single psychotic individual escape the gas chamber. After the war, when I came back to Vienna, I asked what had happened to Dr. J. "He had been imprisoned by the Russians in one of the isolation cells of Steinhof," they told me. "On the next day, however, the door of his cell stood open and Dr. J. was never seen again." Later I was convinced that, like others, he had with the help of his comrades made his way to South America. More recently, however, I was consulted by a former Austrian diplomat who had been imprisoned behind the iron curtain for many years, first in Siberia, and then in the famous Lubanka prison in Moscow. While I was examining him neurologically, he suddenly asked me whether I happened to know Dr. J. After my affirmative reply he continued: "I made his acquaintance in Lubanka. There he died, at about the age of forty, from cancer of the urinary bladder. Before he died, however, he showed himself to be the best comrade you can imagine! He gave consolation to everybody. He lived up to the highest conceivable moral standard. He was the best friend I ever met during my long years in prison!"

This is the story of Dr. J., "the mass murderer of Steinhof." How can you dare to predict the behavior of man! You may predict the movements of a machine, of an automation; more than this, you may even try to predict the mechanisms or "dynamisms" of the human *psyche* as well. But man is more than *psyche*.

Apparently pan-determinism is an infectious disease with which educators have been inoculated, and this is even true of many adherents of religion who are seemingly not aware that thereby they are undermining the very basis of their own convictions. For either man's freedom of decision for or against God, as well as for or against man, must be recognized, or else religion is a delusion, and education an illusion. Freedom is presupposed by both; otherwise they are misconceived.

Freedom, however, is not the last word. Freedom is only part of the story and half of the truth. Freedom is but the negative aspect of the whole phenomenon whose positive aspect is responsibleness. In fact, freedom is in danger of degenerating into mere arbitrariness unless it is lived in terms of responsibleness. That is why *I recommend that the Statue of Liberty on the East Coast be supplemented by a Statue of Responsibility on the West Coast.*

The Psychiatric Credo

There is nothing conceivable which would so condition a man as to leave him without the slightest freedom. Therefore, a residue of freedom, however limited it may be, is left to man in neurotic and even psychotic cases. Indeed, the innermost core of the patient's personality is not even touched by a psychosis. I am reminded of a man of about sixty years of age who was brought to me because of his auditory hallucinations lasting over many decades. I was facing a ruined personality. As it turned out, everyone in his environment regarded him as an idiot. Yet what a strange charm radiated from this man! As a child he had wanted to become a priest. However, he had to be content with the only joy he could experience, and that was singing in the church choir on Sunday mornings. Now, his sister who accompanied him reported that sometimes he grew very excited; yet in the last moment he was always able to regain his self-control. I became interested in the psychodynamics underlying the case, for I thought there was a strong fixation of the patient on his sister; so I asked how he managed to regain his self-control: "For whose sake do you do so?" Thereupon, there was a pause of some seconds, and then the patient answered: "For God's sake." At this moment, the depth of his personality revealed itself, and at the bottom of this depth, irrespective of the poverty of his in-

tellectual endowment, an authentic religious life was dis-
closed.

An incurably psychotic individual may lose his useful-
ness but yet retain the dignity of a human being. This is
my psychiatric credo. Without it I should not think it
worthwhile to be a psychiatrist. For whose sake? Just for
the sake of the damaged brain machine which cannot be
repaired? If the patient were not definitely more, euthanasia would be justified.

Psychiatry Re-humanized

For too long a time, for half a century in fact, psychiatry tried to interpret the human mind merely as a
mechanism, and consequently the therapy of mental disease
merely in terms of a technique. I believe this dream has
been dreamt out. What now begins to loom on the horizon,
are not the sketches of a psychologized medicine but rather
those of a humanized psychiatry.

A doctor, however, who would still interpret his own
role mainly as that of a technician, would confess that he
sees in his patient nothing more than a machine, instead of
seeing the human being behind the disease!

A human being is not one thing among others; *things*
determine each other, but *man* is ultimately self-determining. What he becomes—within the limits of endowment
and environment—he has made out of himself. In the concentration camps, for example, in this living laboratory
and on this testing ground we watched and witnessed some
of our comrades behave like swine while others behaved
like saints. Man has both potentialities within himself;

which one is actualized depends on decisions but not on conditions.

Our generation is realistic for we have come to know man as he really is. After all, man is that being who has invented the gas chambers of Auschwitz; however, he is also that being who has entered those gas chambers upright, with the Lord's Prayer or the *Shema Yisrael* on his lips.

English Bibliography
of Logotherapy and Existenzanalyse

1. BOOKS

Crumbaugh, James C.: *Everything to Gain: A Guide to Self-fulfillment Through Logoanalysis.* Chicago: Nelson-Hall, 1973.

Fabry, Joseph B.: *The Pursuit of Meaning: Logotherapy Applied to Life.* Preface by Viktor E. Frankl. Boston: Beacon Press, 1968; Paperback edition: *A Guide to the Theory and Application of Viktor E. Frankl's Logotherapy,* 1969.

Frankl, Viktor E.: *Man's Search for Meaning: An Introduction to Logotherapy.* Preface by Gordon W. Allport. Boston: Beacon Press, 1962; Paperback edition, New York: Pocket Books, 1973.

————: *The Doctor and the Soul: From Psychotherapy to Logotherapy.* New York: Alfred A. Knopf, Inc.; second, expanded edition, 1965; Paperback edition, New York: Vintage Books, 1973.

————: *Psychotherapy and Existentialism: Selected Papers on Logotherapy.* New York: Washington Square Press, 1967; Clarion paperback, 1968.

————: *The Will to Meaning: Foundations and Applications of Logotherapy.* New York and Cleveland; The World Publishing Company, 1969.

Leslie, Robert C.: *Jesus and Logotherapy: The Ministry of Jesus as Interpreted Through the Psychotherapy of Viktor Frankl.* New York and Nashville: Abingdon Press, 1965; Paperback edition, 1968.

Tweedie, Donald F.: *Logotherapy and the Christian Faith: An Evaluation of Frankl's Existential Approach to Psychotherapy.* Preface by Viktor E. Frankl. Grand Rapids, Mich.: Baker Book House, 1961; Paperback edition, 1965.

————: *The Christian and the Couch: An Introduction to Christian Logotherapy.* Grand Rapids, Mich.: Baker Book House, 1963.

Ungersma, Aaron J.: *The Search for Meaning: A New Approach in Psychotherapy and Pastoral Psychology.* Philadelphia: Westminster Press, 1961; Paperback edition, Foreword by Viktor E. Frankl, 1968.

2. CHAPTERS IN BOOKS

Arnold, Magda B., and John A. Gasson: "Logotherapy and Existential Analysis," in *The Human Person,* New York: Ronald Press, 1954.

Barnitz, Harry W.: "Frankl's Logotherapy," in *Existentialism and the New Christianity.* New York: Philosophical Library, 1969.

Frankl, Viktor E.: contributions to *Critical Incidents in Psychotherapy,* edited by S. W. Standal and R. J. Corsini. Englewood Cliffs, New Jersey: Prentice-Hall, 1959.

————: "Fragments from the Logotherapeutic Treatment of Four Cases. With an Introduction and Epilogue by G. Kaczanowski," in *Modern Psychotherapeutic Practice: Innovations in Technique,* edited by Arthur Burton. Palo Alto, California: Science and Behavior Books, 1965.

————: "The Task of Education in an Age of Meaninglessness," in *New Prospects for the Small Liberal Arts College,* edited by Sidney S. Letter. New York: Teachers College Press, 1968.

————: "Reductionism and Nihilism," in *Beyond Reductionism: New Perspectives in the Life Sciences (The Alpbach Symposium 1698),* edited by Arthur Koestler and J. R. Smythies. New York: Macmillan, 1970.

————: "Universities and the Quest for Peace," in *Report of the First World Conference on the Role of the University in the Quest for Peace.* Binghamton, New York: State University of New York, 1970.

————: "Youth in Search of Meaning." In *Students Search for Meaning,* edited by James Edward Doty. Kansas City, Missouri: The Lowell Press, 1971.

Freilicher, M.: "Applied Existential Psychology: Viktor Frankl and Logotherapy," in *PsychoSources,* edited by Evelyn Shapiro. New York: Bantam Books, 1973.

Ledermann, E. K.: "Viktor E. Frankl's Ontological Value Ethics," in *Existential Neurosis,* London: Butterworths, 1972.

Leslie, Robert: "Frankl's New Concept of Man," in *Contemporary Religious Issues,* edited by Donald E. Hartsock. Belmont, California: Wadsworth Publishing Company, 1968.

Liston, Robert A.: "Viktor Frankl," in *Healing the Mind: Eight Views of Human Nature.* New York: Praeger, 1974.

Marks, Isaac M.: "Paradoxical Intention ('Logotherapy')," in *Fears and Phobias,* New York: Academic Press, 1969.

————: "Paradoxical Intention," in *Behavior Modification,* edited by W. Stewart Agras. Boston: Little, Brown and Company, 1972.

Maslow, Abraham H.: "Comments on Dr. Frankl's Paper," in *Readings in Humanistic Psychology,* edited by Anthony J. Sutich and Miles A. Vich. New York: The Free Press, 1969.

McKinney, Fred: "Man's Search for Meaning," in *Psychology in Action.* New York: Macmillan, 1967.

Misiak, Henry, and Virginia Staudt Sexton: "Logotherapy," in *Phenomenological, Existential, and Humanistic Psychologies: A Historical Survey.* New York: Grune and Stratton, 1973.

Patterson, C. H.: "Frankl's Logotherapy," in *Theories of Counseling and Psychotherapy.* New York: Harper and Row, 1966.

Salit, Norman: "Existential Analyses; Logotherapy—the Gulf Narrows," in *The Worlds of Norman Salit,* edited by Abraham Burstein. New York: Bloch, 1966.

Schneider, Marius G.: "The Existentialistic Concept of the Human Person in Viktor E. Frankl's Logotherapy," in *Studies in Philosophy and the History of Philosophy,* edited by John K. Ryan. Washington: Catholic University of America Press, 1974.

Spiegelberg, Herbert: "Viktor Frankl: Phenomenology in Logotherapy and *Existenzanalyse,*" in *Phenomenology in Psychology and Psychiatry.* Evanston: Northwestern University Press, 1972.

Strunk, Orlo: "Religious Maturity and Viktor E. Frankl," in *Mature Religion.* New York and Nashville: Abingdon Press, 1965.

Vanderveldt, James H., and Robert P. Odenwald: "Existential Analysis," in *Psychiatry and Catholicism.* New York: McGraw-Hill, 1952.

Zavalloni, Roberto: "Human Freedom and Logotherapy," in *Self-Determination.* Chicago: Forum Books, 1962.

3. ARTICLES AND MISCELLANEOUS*

Ansbacher, Rowena R.: "The Third Viennese School of Psychotherapy." *Journal of Individual Psychology,* XV (1959), 236–37.

Ballard, R. E.: "An Empirical Investigation of Viktor Frankl's Concept of the Search for Meaning: A Pilot Study with a Sample of Tuberculosis Patients." Doctoral Dissertation, Michigan State University, 1965.

Birnbaum, Ferdinand: "Frankl's Existential Psychology from the Viewpoint of Individual Psychology." *Journal of Individual Psychology,* XVII (1961), 162–66.

Bordeleau, Louis-Gabriel: "La relation entre les valeurs du choix vocationnel et les valeurs créatrices chez V. E. Frankl." Doctoral dissertation presented to the Department of Psychology, The University of Ottawa (Ontario, Canada), 1971.

Bulka, Reuven P.: "An Analysis of the Viability of Frankl's Logotherapeutic System as a Secular Theory." Thesis presented to the Department of Religious Studies of the University of Ottawa as partial fulfillment of the requirements for the degree of Master of Arts, 1969.

————: "Denominational Implications of the Religious Nature of Logotherapy." Thesis presented to the Department of Religious Studies of the University of Ottawa as partial fulfillment of the requirements for the degree of Doctor of Philosophy. Ottawa, Canada, 1971.

————: "Logotherapy and Judaism—Some Philosophical Comparisons." *Tradition,* XII (1972), 72–89.

————: "Logotherapy and Judaism." *Jewish Spectator,* XXXVII, no. 7 (September 1972), 17–19.

* Denotes works appearing in *Psychotherapy and Existentialism: Selected Papers on Logotherapy.* New York: Washington Square Press, 1967.

————: "Death in Life—Talmudic and Logotherapeutic Affirmations." *Humanitas (Journal of the Institute of Man)*, X, no. 1 (February 1974), 33–42.

————: "The Ecumenical Ingredient in Logotherapy." *Journal of Ecumenical Studies*, XI, no. 1 (Winter 1974), 13–24.

Burck, James Lester: "The Relevance of Viktor Frankl's 'Will to Meaning' for Preaching to Juvenile Delinquents." A Master of Theology thesis submitted to the Southern Baptist Theological Seminary, Louisville, Kentucky, 1966.

Calabrese, Edward James: "The Evolutionary Basis of Logotherapy." Dissertation, University of Massachusetts, 1974.

Cavanagh, Michael E.: "The Relationship Between Frankl's 'Will to Meaning' and the Discrepancy Between the Actual Self and the Ideal Self." Doctoral Dissertation, University of Ottawa, Canada, 1966.

Crumbaugh, James C.: "The Application of Logotherapy." *Journal of Existentialism*, V (1965), 403–12.

————: "Cross Validation of Purpose-in-Life Test Based on Frankl's Concepts." *Journal of Individual Psychology*, XXIV (1968), 74–81.

————: "Frankl's Logotherapy: A New Orientation in Counseling." *Journal of Religion and Health*, X (1971), 373–86.

————: "Changes in Frankl's Existential Vacuum as a Measure of Therapeutic Outcome." *Newsletter for Research in Psychology* (Veterans Administration Center, Bay Pines, Florida), vol. 14, no. 2, May 1972, 35–37.   ————

————: "Frankl's Logotherapy: An Answer to the Crisis in Identity." *Newsletter of the Mississippi Personnel and Guidance Association*, IV, no. 2 (October 1972), 3.

————: "Aging and Adjustment: The Applicability of Logotherapy and the Purpose-in-Life Test." *The Gerontologist*, XII (1972), 418–20.

————, and Leonard T. Maholick: "The Case for Frankl's 'Will to Meaning.'" *Journal of Existential Psychiatry*, IV (1963), 43–8.

————: "An Experimental Study in Existentialism: The Psychometric Approach to Frankl's Concept of *Noögenic Neurosis*." *Journal of Clinical Psychology*, XX (1964), 200–7.

————: Sister Mary Raphael, and Raymond R. Shrader: "Frankl's Will to Meaning in a Religious Order" (delivered before Division 24, American Psychological Association, at the annual convention in San Francisco, August 30, 1968). *Journal of Clinical Psychology,* XXVI (1970), 206–7.

Dansart, Bernard: "Development of a Scale to Measure Attitudinal Values as Defined by Viktor Frankl." Dissertation, Northern Illinois University, 1974.

Dickson, Charles W.: "Logotherapy and the Redemptive Encounter." *Dialogue,* Spring 1974, 110–114.

Duncan, Franklin D.: "Logotherapy and the Pastoral Care of Physically Disabled Persons." A thesis in the Department of Psychology of Religion submitted to the faculty of the Graduate School of Theology in partial fulfillment of the requirements for the degree of Master of Theology at Southern Baptist Theological Seminary, 1968.

Fabry, Joseph: "A Most Ingenious Paradox." *The Register-Leader of the Unitarian Universalist Association,* vol. 149 (June 1967), 7–8.

————, and Max Knight (pseudonym Peter Fabrizius): "Viktor Frankl's Logotherapy." *Delphian Quarterly,* XLVII, no. 3 (1964), 27–30.

————: "The Use of Humor in Therapy." *Delphian Quarterly,* XLVIII, no. 3 (1965), 22–36.

Forstmeyer, Annemarie von: "The Will to Meaning as a Prerequisite for Self-Actualization." A Thesis Presented to the Faculty of California Western University in Partial Fulfillment of the Requirements for the Degree Master of Arts, 1968.

Fox, Douglas A.: "Logotherapy and Religion." *Religion in Life,* XXXI (1965), 235–44.

Frankl, Viktor E.: "Logos and Existence in Psychotherapy." *American Journal of Psychotherapy,* VII (1953), 8–15.

————: "Guest Editorial." *Academy Reporter,* III, no. 5 (May 1958), 1–4.

————: "On Logotherapy and Existential Analysis" (paper read before the Association for the Advancement of Psychoanalysis, New York, April 17, 1957). *American Journal of Psychoanalysis,* XVIII (1958), 28–37.

————: "The Search for Meaning." *Saturday Review,* September 13, 1958.

————: "Religion and Existential Psychotherapy." *Gordon Review,* VI (1961), 2–10.

————: "Psychotherapy and Philosophy." *Philosophy Today,* V (1961), 59–64.

————: "The Depersonalization of Sex." *Synthesis (The Realization of the Self),* I, no. 1, Spring 1974, 7–11.

————: "In Steady Search for Meaning." *Liberal Dimension,* II, no. 2 (1964), 3–8.

————: "Logotherapy and Existential Analysis: A Review" (paper read before the Symposium on Logotherapy, 6th International Congress of Psychotherapy, London, August 26, 1964) *American Journal of Psychotherapy,* XX (1966), 252–60.

————: "Time and Responsibility." *Existential Psychiatry,* I (1966), 361–66.

————: "What Is a Man?" *Life Association News,* LXII, no. 9 (September 1967), 151–57.

————: "Logotherapy." *The Israel Annals of Psychiatry and Related Disciplines,* VII (1967), 142–55.

————: "Experiences in a Concentration Camp." *Jewish Heritage,* XI (1968), 5–7.

————: "The Search for Meaning" (abstract from a series of lectures given at the Brandeis Institute in California). *Jewish Heritage,* XI (1968), 8–11.

————: "The Cosmos and the Mind. (How Far Can We Go?) A Dialogue with Geoffrey Frost." *Pace,* V, no. 3 (August 1969), 34–9.

————: "Fore-Runner of Existential Psychiatry." *Journal of Individual Psychology,* XXVI (1970), 12.

————: "Entering the Human Dimension." *Attitude,* I (1970), 2–6.

————: "Determinism and Humanism." *Humanitas (Journal of the Institute of Man),* VII (1971), 23–36.

————: "The Feeling of Meaninglessness: A Challenge to Psychotherapy." *The American Journal of Psychoanalysis,* XXXII, no. I (1972), 85–9.

————: "Man in Search of Meaning." *Widening Horizons* (Rockford College), vol. 8, no. 5, August 1972.

————: "Encounter: The Concept and Its Vulgarization." *The Journal of the American Academy of Psychoanalysis*, I, no. I (1973), 73–83.

Gerz, Hans O.: "The Treatment of the Phobic and the Obsessive-Compulsive Patient Using Paradoxical Intention sec. Viktor E. Frankl." *Journal of Neuropsychiatry*, III, no. 6 (July–August 1962), 375–87.

————: "Experience with the Logotherapeutic Technique of Paradoxical Intention in the Treatment of Phobic and Obsessive-Compulsive Patients" (paper read at the Symposium of Logotherapy at the 6th International Congress of Psychotherapy, London, England, August 1964). *American Journal of Psychiatry*, CXXIII, no. 5 (November 1966), 548–53.

————: "Reply." *American Journal of Psychiatry*, CXXIII, no. 10 (April 1967), 1306.

Green, Herman H.: "The 'Existential Vacuum' and the Pastoral Care of Elderly Widows in a Nursing Home." Master's thesis, Southern Baptist Theological Seminary, Louisville, Kentucky, 1970.

Grollman, Earl A.: "Viktor E. Frankl: A Bridge Between Psychiatry and Religion." *Conservative Judaism*, XIX, no. 1 (Fall 1964), 19–23.

————: "The Logotherapy of Viktor E. Frankl." *Judaism*, XIV (1965), 22–38.

Grossman, Nathan: "The Rabbi and the Doctor of the Soul." *Jewish Spectator*, XXXIV, no. I (January 1969), 8–12.

Gulbrandsen, Francis Aloysius: "Some of the Pedagogical Implications in the Theoretical Work of Viktor Frankl in Existential Psychology: A Study in the Philosophic Foundations of Education." Doctoral Dissertation, Michigan State University, 1972.

Hall, Mary Harrington: "A Conversation with Viktor Frankl of Vienna." *Psychology Today*, I, no. 9 (February 1968), 56–63.

Harrington, Donald Szantho: "The View from the Existential Vacuum," *Academy Reporter*, IX, no. 9 (December 1964), 1–4.

Havens, Leston L.: "Paradoxical Intention." *Psychiatry and Social Science Review*, II (1968), 16–19.

Haworth, D. Swan: "Viktor Frankl." *Judaism,* XIV (1965), 351–2.

Henderson, J. T.: "The Will to Meaning of Viktor Frankl as a Meaningful Factor of Personality." A Master's thesis, The University of Maryland, 1970.

Holmes, R. M.: "Meaning and Responsibility: A Comparative Analysis of the Concept of the Responsible Self in Search of Meaning in the Thought of Viktor Frankl and H. Richard Niebuhr with Certain Implications for the Church's Ministry to the University." Doctoral Dissertation, Pacific School of Religion, 1965.

————: "Alcoholics Anonymous as Group Logotherapy." *Pastoral Psychology,* XXI (1970), 30–36.

Hyman, William: "Practical Aspects of Logotherapy in Neurosurgery." *Existential Psychiatry,* VII (1969), 99–101.

Johnson, Paul E.: "Logotherapy: A Corrective for Determinism." *Christian Advocate,* V (November 23, 1961), 12–13.

————: "The Challenge of Logotherapy." *Journal of Religion and Health,* VII (1968), 122–30.

————: "Meet Doctor Frankl." *Adult Student,* XXIV (October 1964), 8–10.

————: "The Meaning of Logotherapy." *Adult Student,* XXVI, no. 8 (April 1967), 4–5.

Jones, Elbert Whaley: "Nietzsche and Existential-Analysis." Dissertation in the Department of Philosophy submitted to the faculty of the Graduate School of Arts and Science in partial fulfillment of the requirements for the degree of Master of Arts, New York University, 1967.

Kaczanowski, Godfryd: "Frankl's Logotherapy." *American Journal of Psychiatry,* CXVII (1960), 563.

————: "Logotherapy—A New Psychotherapeutic Tool," *Psychosomatics,* vol. 8 (May-June 1967), 158–61.

Klapper, Naomi: "On Being Human: A Comparative Study of Abraham J. Heschel and Viktor Frankl." Doctoral Dissertation, Jewish Theological Seminary of America, 1973.

Klitzke, Louis L.: "Students in Emerging Africa: Humanistic Psychology and Logotherapy in Tanzania," *Journal of Humanistic Psychology,* IX (1969), 105–26.

Kosukegawa, Tsugio: "A Comparative Study of the Differences Between Christian Existence and Secular Existence, and of Their Existential Frustration." *Japanese Journal of Educational and Social Psychology,* VII, no. 2 (1968), 195–208.

Lapinsohn, Leonard I.: "Relationship of the Logotherapeutic Concepts of Anticipatory Anxiety and Paradoxical Intention to the Neurophysiological Theory of Induction." *Behavioral Neuropsychiatry,* III, no. 3–4 (1971), 12–14 and 24.

Leslie, Robert C.: "Viktor E. Frankl's New Concept of Man." *Motive,* XXII (1962), 16–19.

Marrer, Robert F.: "Existential-Phenomenological Foundations in Logotherapy Applicable to Counseling." Dissertation, Ohio University, 1972.

Maslow, A. H.: "Comments on Dr. Frankl's Paper." *Journal of Humanistic Psychology,* VI (1966), 107–12.

Meier, Augustine: "Frankl's 'Will to Meaning' as Measured by the Purpose-in-Life Test in Relation to Age and Sex Differences." Dissertation presented to the University of Ottawa, Canada 1973.

Mullenberg, Don T.: "Meaning in Life: Its Significance in Psychotherapy." A dissertation presented to the faculty of the Graduate School, University of Missouri, 1968.

Müller-Hegemann, D.: "Methodological Approaches in Psychotherapy: Current Concepts in East Germany." *American Journal of Psychotherapy,* XVII (1963), 554–68.

Murphy, Leonard: "Extent of Purpose-in-Life and Four Frankl Proposed Life Objectives." Doctoral Dissertation in Department of Psychology, The University of Ottawa (Ontario, Canada), 1967. (Thesis no. 295 in Library.)

Murphy, Maribeth L.: "Viktor Frankl: The New Phenomenology of Meaning." *The U.S.I.U. Doctoral Society Journal,* III, no. 2 (June 1970), 1–10, and IV, no. 1 (Winter 1970–71), 45–46.

Newton, Joseph R.: "Therapeutic Paradoxes, Paradoxical Intentions, and Negative Practice." *American Journal of Psychotherapy,* XXII (1968), 68–81.

O'Connell, Walter E.: "Viktor Frankl, the Adlerian?" *Psychiatric Spectator,* vol. VI, no. 11, 1970, 13–14.

————: "Frankl, Adler, and Spirituality." *Journal of Religion and Health,* XI (1972), 134–38.

"Originator of Logotherapy Discusses Its Basic Premises" (Interview). *Roche Report: Frontiers of Clinical Psychiatry,* vol. 5, no. 1 (January 1, 1968) 5–6.

Pervin, Lawrence A.: "Existentialism, Psychology, and Psychotherapy." *American Psychologist,* XV (1960), 305–9.

Polak, Paul: "Frankl's Existential Analysis." *American Journal of Psychotherapy,* III (1949), 517–22.

Richmond, Bert O., Robert L. Mason, and Virginia Smith: "Existential Frustration and Anomie." *J. Women's Deans and Counselors* (Spring 1969).

Rowland, Stanley J., Jr.: "Viktor Frankl and the Will to Meaning." *Christian Century,* LXXIX (June 6, 1962), 722–24.

Sahakian, William S., and Barbara Jacquelyn Sahakian: "Logotherapy as a Personality Theory." *The Israel Annals of Psychiatry and Related Disciplines,* X (1972), 230–44.

Sargent, George Andrew: "Job Satisfaction, Job Involvement and Purpose in Life: A Study of Work and Frankl's Will to Meaning." A Thesis Presented to the Faculty of the United States International University in Partial Fulfillment of the Requirements for the Degree Master of Arts, 1971.

————: "Motivation and Meaning: Frankl's Logotherapy in the Work Situation." Dissertation, United States International University, 1973.

Schachter, Stanley J.: "Bettelheim and Frankl: Contradicting Views of the Holocaust." *Reconstructionist,* XXVI, no. 20 (February 10, 1961), 6–11.

Solyom, L., J. Garza-Perez, B. L. Ledwige, and C. Solyom: "Paradoxical Intention in the Treatment of Obsessive Thoughts: A Pilot Study." *Comprehensive Psychiatry,* vol. 13, no. 3 (May 1972), 291–97.

"The Doctor and the Soul. Dr. Viktor Frankl." *Harvard Medical Alumni Bulletin,* XXXVI, no. 1 (Fall 1961), 8.

"The Father of Logotherapy." *Existential Psychiatry,* vol. I (1967), 439.

Turner, R. H.: "Comment on Dr. Frankl's Paper." *Journal of Existential Psychiatry,* I (1960), 21–3.

Victor, Ralph G., and Carolyn M. Krug: " 'Paradoxical Intention' in the Treatment of Compulsive Gambling." *American Journal of Psychotherapy,* XXI, no. 4 (October 1967), 808–14.

"Viktor Frankl." *The Colby Alumnus,* LI (Spring 1962), 5.

Waugh, Robert J. L.: "Paradoxical Intention." *American Journal of Psychiatry,* vol. 123, no. 10 (April 1967), 1305–6.

Weiss, M. David: "Frankl's Approach to the Mentally Ill." *Association of Mental Hospital Chaplains' Newsletter* (Fall 1962), 39–42.

Weisskopf-Joelson, Edith: "Logotherapy and Existential Analysis." *Acta Psychotherapeutica,* VI (1958), 193–204.

————: "Paranoia and the Will-to-Meaning." *Existential Psychiatry,* I (1966), 316–20.

————: "Some Suggestions Concerning the Concept of Awareness." *Psychotherapy: Theory, Research and Practice,* VIII (1971), 2–7.

Yeates, J. W.: "The Educational Implications of the Logotherapy of Viktor E. Frankl." Doctoral Dissertation, University of Mississippi, 1968.

4. FILMS, RECORDS AND TAPES

Frankl, Viktor E.: "Logotherapy," a film produced by the Department of Psychiatry, Neurology, and Behavioral Sciences, University of Oklahoma Medical School.

————: "Frankl and the Search for Meaning," a film produced by Psychological Films, 205 West Twentieth Street, Santa Ana, California 92706.

————: "Youth in Search of Meaning," a videotape produced by the Youth Corps and Metro Cable Television. Contact: Youth Corps, 56 Bond Street, Toronto, Ontario M5B 1k2, Canada.

————: "Human Freedom and Meaning in Life," and "Self-Transcendence—Therapeutic Agent in Sexual Neurosis," videotapes. Copies of the tapes can be ordered for a service fee. Address inquiries to the Manager, Learning Resource Distribution Center, United States International University, San Diego, California 92131.

————: Three Lectures on Logotherapy, given at the Brandeis Institute, Brandeis, California 93064. Longplaying records.

————: "Man in Search of Meaning: Two Dialogues, Self-Transcendence: The Motivational Theory of Logotherapy," "What Is Meant by Meaning?" and "Logotherapy and Existentialism," audiotapes produced by Sound Seminars, College Division, McGraw-Hill Book Company, P.O. Box 402, Hightstown, New Jersey 08520.

————: "The Existential Vacuum" ("Existential Frustration As a Challenge to Psychiatry"—"Logotherapy As a Concept of Man"—"Logotherapy As a Philosophy of Life"), tapes produced by Argus Communication, 3505 North Ashland Avenue, Chicago, Illinois 60657.

————: "The Existential Vacuum: A Challenge to Psychiatry. Address given at The Unitarian Church, San Francisco, California, October 13, 1969." A tape produced by Big Sur Recordings, 2015 Bridgeway, Sausalito, California 94965.

————: "Meaninglessness: Today's Dilemma," an audiotape produced by Creative Resources, 4800 West Waco Drive, Waco, Texas 76703.

————: "Man's Search for Meaning. An Introduction to Logotherapy." Recording for the Blind, Inc., 215 East 58th Street, New York, New York 10022.

————: "Youth in Search of Meaning." Word Cassette Library, 4800 West Waco Drive, Waco, Texas 76703 ($4.98).

————, and Huston Smith: "Value Dimensions in Teaching," a color television film produced by Hollywood Animators, Inc., for the California Junior College Association. Rental or purchase through Dr. Rex Wignall, Director, Chaffey College, Alta Loma, California.

"The Humanistic Revolution: Pioneers in Perspective," interviews with leading humanistic psychologists: Abraham Maslow, Gardner Murphy, Carl Rogers, Rollo May, Paul Tillich, Frederick Perls, Viktor Frankl, Alan Watts. Psychological Films, 205 West 20th Street, Santa Ana, California 92706. Sale $250; rental $20.

ABOUT THE AUTHOR

Viktor E. Frankl is Professor of Neurology and Psychiatry at the University of Vienna Medical School, Professor of Logotherapy at U.S. International University, Visiting Clinical Professor of Psychiatry at Stanford University, President of the Austrian Medical Society of Psychotherapy and has been visiting professor at Harvard University, Duquesne University and Southern Methodist University.

Born in 1905, Dr. Frankl received the degrees of Doctor of Medicine and Doctor of Philosophy from the University of Vienna. During World War II he spent three years at Auschwitz, Dachau and other concentration camps.

The leading figure in what has come to be called the Third Viennese School of Psychotherapy, Dr. Frankl first published in 1924 at the invitation of Sigmund Freud in the *International Journal of Psychoanalysis*. He has since published twenty books, which have been translated into Spanish, Italian, English, Japanese, Dutch, Swedish, Polish, Norwegian, Danish, French, Chinese, Hebrew, Portuguese and Greek, and has published extensively in psychiatry journals throughout the world. Dr. Frankl has been guest lecturer at the Royal Society of Medicine in London and in Argentina, Australia, Ceylon, China, Costa Rica, India, Israel, Japan, Hawaii, Mexico, Puerto Rico and South Africa. He has made forty lecture tours throughout the United States.